THE TRUTH SHALL SET YOU FREE

By the same author:

Soul Sista: How to be a Girl of God! (Hodder & Stoughton, 2000)

The Truth Shall Set You Free

BETH REDMAN

survivor

First published 2003
Reprinted 2004

ISBN 1 84291 159 7

Published by
KINGSWAY COMMUNICATIONS LTD
Lottbridge Drove, Eastbourne BN23 6NT, England.
Email: books@kingsway.co.uk

Book design and production for the publishers by
Bookprint Creative Services, P.O. Box 827, BN21 3YJ, England.
Printed in the USA.

Contents

Dedication

For Anna Emilia DeFelippo –
a true and faithful friend,
a constant encouragement and support,
my beautiful soul sista; I love you x

Thanks

First of all I want to thank my husband Matt, who has always encouraged me, loved me and spurred me on. He willingly put his life on hold to support me writing this book. Matt, there is no one else like you – Maisey, Noah and I are so blessed by your love and your true heart for God. Thank you xxx

Thanks to my two gorgeous babies for being patient and going with the flow while I was up in the attic writing for hours on end! Massive thanks and appreciation to Corin D'enno for Wednesdays and to Rachel and Jo at Elm House for the morning sessions!

Mike Pilavachi – once again you have supported me in writing this book and running with the vision of Soul Sista. I am so grateful that you are for me and behind me. You are my family and my faithful friend, and we love you very much!

Tim Hughes – our little brother – thanks for your

encouragement and for your friendship. We are very proud of you.

Thank you to Les Moir and John Pac at Kingsway for getting behind the book and for all the hours of encouragement you have put in, with special appreciation to David Maloney at Hodder & Stoughton.

Don Williams – I am so grateful for your wisdom and your vast knowledge of the Bible. You put in many hours for me. Thanks.

Sarah Adams – thanks for going above and beyond your job description.

Thanks to Andi Smith for the brilliant drawings.

To Vicky Beeching and the girls on the Soul Sista board: Ali, Andreana, Rachel and Bee. Thank you for your support, your time and your vulnerability – you are faithful and beautiful girls of God.

Finally, to my two soul sistas-in-law – Ellie and Sarah. I love the way you have persevered and followed after God . . . you inspire me and I thank God I am part of your family.

Beth Redman

Intros from the Boys

In one way I'm totally unqualified to write an intro to this book for 'Soul Sistas'. I do have a wife, a daughter and two younger sisters, but I'd still never dare to claim that I understand women!

On the other hand, my wife, Beth, is very well equipped to write on this subject. First, and most importantly, she has an inspiring passion for God. And second she lives with a strong desire to see young women today grow in the truth and ways of God. Ever since I met Beth she's been a listening ear to many young women and often seems to be offering godly and timely advice to those she meets with. So I'm delighted that some of this same guidance now gets to make it into a book too.

This is a tough world for a young woman to grow up in. Life today seems to be crammed full of pressures, temptations and knock-downs for the average girl. I've witnessed some of the challenges for a Soul Sista today, in the lives of Beth, my sisters Ellie and Sarah and, even more frighteningly, our little daughter. I've come across others who've been completely thrown off course by the pressures of today's image-consumed and soul-burdening society. In some ways it's a pretty bleak situation. But there is a truth that can set us free. In this book Beth takes Soul Sistas everywhere on a quest to pursue that beautiful truth – the incredible word of God.

I am so proud of Beth for pouring her heart out in this way. There were many early mornings and late nights spent writing, as she faithfully juggled the balance of being a wife, a mother and an author. God has entrusted Beth with a fantastic gift to communicate the wisdom and passion he has placed in her heart. I pray she will inspire you in your walk with God as much as she has inspired me in mine.

Matt Redman

I've always found Beth to be honest, caring, passionate and great fun. There's never a dull moment with her. In this book I find the exact same qualities. As I sat down to read it I was intrigued to know what I'd learn about the ways of women. What I found was a down-to-earth, practical and honest book about living life as a girl for God. Here are words of wisdom and encouragement that help face those tough issues that life throws at us.

Personally I found it to be very helpful and inspiring. There's stuff in this book that all men should read about. I remember when reading Beth's first book, *How to be a Girl of God*, I felt the need to make up some excuse about why I was reading it. I think I said it was for research purposes! Well, guys, if you need to, make up an excuse. Buy it for your sister and read it first. There are truths within this book that need to be heard and acted upon. You can't read this book without being challenged. It provokes a response. That can at times be uncomfortable, but it's necessary as we open ourselves to be changed more into Christ's likeness.

The thing I loved most about this book though was that it left you in no doubt where the answers to life lie. This book is unashamedly about God: his heart for us, his love and mercy shown to us, and his promises made to us. It's the truth of knowing God that will heal us and ultimately bring contentment and peace to our lives. After reading this book I was left first and foremost thinking, what an awesome and wonderful God we serve.

Tim Hughes

This is a great book. Like its author it is honest, funny and full of insight. Beth has been a close friend for a number of years. She is passionate in her pursuit of God. She has a love of the Bible that is infectious. She is also blessed with a frightening dose of what I can only describe as women's intuition. Sometimes I have wondered if she has my mind bugged. I'm sure she often knows what I'm feeling before I do!

This book is Beth all over. She tells it as it is. She can do this with integrity because she has known pain in her own life, but also through the pain she has found God, his truth and his healing. Because Beth loves the Bible she knows how much God's words can change lives. God's word is all over this book and that is why I am convinced it will set many girls free. While it is really important to know that people understand us, and while good advice is precious and counselling very helpful, in the end only the truth sets us free.

This is such an encouraging book because it is packed with truth. In a world where we are lied to and manipulated into believing things about ourselves that are destructive, this book will, I believe, be life-changing to thousands of girls. Like its author, it is vulnerable and compassionate. Again, like its author, it is inspiring, encouraging and extremely practical, because it always points to the God who is the way, the truth and the life.

I love *The Truth Shall Set You Free* and I am sure you will too.

Mike Pilavachi

Welcome to the Truth

Teenage problem pages receive hundreds of letters every week. Desperate young girls asking huge questions about themselves, their struggles, their sexuality, their family and their pain – 'Why does this happen?' 'What should I do?' 'Who can I turn to?' And so the faithful agony aunts dish out their advice, sometimes leaving an address or a phone number. Generally though that's the last you'll hear from them. They don't write or phone – you are on your own.

God has written the most incredible answers to our

problem-page letters. If we choose to read them we can expect to find direct answers in times of need and a personal message of love, grace, wisdom and affirmation. The Bible brings tender truth and powerful answers in times of pain and confusion. God has given us many amazing gifts: not only his Son Jesus and his Holy Spirit, but also his word – the Bible – a book we can hold in our hands to hear straight from his heart and mind.

The Bible, our manual for life

As a teenage girl today it is so easy to lose the way. We are entertained by television and magazines, gossip and chatter. All of these things are distractions. They cause us to fill our days with everything but God and the result is many find themselves living in an unsatisfied state.

Matt and I had just moved to a new area and were for ever getting lost. Fortunately we had use of a car with a built-in satellite navigation system. All we needed to do was type in where we wanted to go and the car spoke out directions till we reached our destination. This system was an amazing tool that stopped us from getting lost again!

That is just like the Bible. God has given us a book full of powerful wisdom and advice. It is not out of date or irrelevant – in fact there is stuff in there for every situation you may face as a young girl today. But where do you start and how do you find this truth?

If you were lost in London, you wouldn't just randomly open your A–Z and expect it to direct you. To use the A–Z effectively you would find out where you needed to go and see what the book had to say about it. It is the same for the Bible. Although sometimes you can flip open a page and find an answer to a problem, it is more helpful to find out which particular chapter or verse contains the advice or help you need.

Later on in this book we will take a look at which verses in the Bible to read when you are struggling in a particular situation and also how to actually make time to read it every day. Many of us race around in the morning trying on several different outfits, applying lip-gloss and stuffing in a slice of toast and Marmite before quickly saying, 'Oh yes, and God please bless my day' – and that is our quiet time! We will face many things during that day – unfortunately not just success and laughter but possibly temptation, hurt, selfishness, disappointment and stress. And we will need more than just that quick fix to get us through.

Several years ago I was in a horrible dilemma. Suddenly I felt a strong tug to go to my room and pick up my Bible. I remember thinking out loud, 'But what should I read?' I opened it to the book of Romans, which I was reading through that week, and my eyes were drawn to a passage that nearly knocked me off my feet. It was as if God had written me a personal letter about my exact situation and what I should do about it. God had spoken directly to me through a book that was written nearly 2,000 years ago and yet its words are powerful and true for today.

I became aware that I lived my life taking advice from everyone but God. I took my Bible with me occasionally to the meeting on a Sunday, or flicked through it just before I nodded off to sleep, but I had never really used it in the way it was meant. Psalm 119:105 says, 'Your word is a lamp to my feet' – it brings light and life, clarity and power. From that day on I have not been able to look at the Bible in the same way.

Recently, just before our second baby was born, we found ourselves in a stressful dilemma. We had returned from a short spell in America and were preparing to relocate from Watford to the south. Unfortunately our housing plans went a bit pear-shaped and the house we were going for fell through again and again. We ended up moving seven times, from one temporary place to another, not only confusing our toddler but also causing us to feel unsettled and confused. Almost eight months into my pregnancy we moved back to Watford, feeling worn out and disillusioned. Soon after that our baby son, Noah Luca, arrived. He was four weeks early and came out struggling for breath. The doctors moved him immediately to intensive care, where he remained in a critical condition for several days.

Many people gave us support and counsel, but the place we gained the most strength from was the Bible. One verse I read in Joshua said, 'I will never leave you nor forsake you.' I knew that God was saying to me, 'I am right with you and I am staying with you in this hard time.' Just as Noah was being born Matt saw a huge rainbow in the sky. At the time I didn't really appreciate the information! But afterwards, when Noah was really ill in intensive care, I read a verse from Genesis that said, 'God put a rainbow in the sky as a sign of his promise to Noah.' I felt God was using this verse to reassure me that Noah was going to be OK.

Miraculously our little boy recovered and we eventually moved into the house that had caused so much stress. I have consistently found in my life that when I turn to God and his word he gives me guidance, and even if it doesn't seem so at the time, he makes my paths straight.

When I was offered the chance to write this book, I jumped at it, not only because I am passionate about encouraging young women in their faith, but also because I believe the Bible is true, and I've experienced it to be true. I hope this book can somehow help to pass on the amazing goodness of God and the wonderful comfort and truth that the Bible brings. For the Bible is not just a textbook, a history book or some sort of Christian self-help manual. It is a powerful weapon in our hands – a sword for truth, freedom, light and life – and it was written for you! So take it off the shelf, blow away the dust and put it to the test.

Read on and rise up as girls of truth!

With much love to you all,

Beth Redman xxx
Soul Sista, Soul Survivor

1
The Truth about Identity

'I like me! I like me! I like me!' Maisey marched around the kitchen with the sort of confidence only a two-year-old has. We laughed as we watched her dancing around singing such a happy song. 'Mummy, I like me,' she said once more before skipping off into the next room. I don't know where this statement came from, but it was sweet to hear what a great self-image our little girl had.

But how long would it last? In the summer our little Maisey wanders round the garden splashing in the paddling pool and playing with her dolls. Her little bottom wobbles as she contentedly skips around without a care in the world. But what if one day she looks down and suddenly doesn't like what she sees? What if she stops 'liking me' and wants to start 'changing me'?

Where does our worth come from?

Recently we went to a friend's baby dedication. Levi Jesse Johnson was only ten days old. He lay in his pram blissfully unaware of all the attention he was getting. I looked across at him and smiled. He was a blank piece of paper, a clean slate. Although his character and his gifts and abilities had already been formed in the womb, his experiences from today on would determine who he was and how he felt about himself.

I was pretty sure his experiences of life were going to be good. Levi is blessed to have two amazing parents who love God and are kind, generous and fair. He also has two sisters and a brother who I know will love and protect him. His extended family is vast and overflowing with decent, godly people. I think he will turn out just fine.

Not everyone is as blessed as Levi. We don't choose the families we are born into. Even if our mums and dads are nice people, highflyers or church leaders that does not guarantee they will make good parents. Whether or not you realise it, the experiences you've had at home and with your parents will determine how you feel about yourself today. Someone who has received affirmation and encouragement from their family will be sure to have a healthy self-image and a strong sense of security, confidence and emotional stability. Mary Pytches says in her book *Who Am I?*:

> No family is perfect but a properly functional family is characterised by parental availability, good communication and uninterrupted loving. The results for the child of such a stable and safe childhood will be a healthy perception of the world and, most importantly, a healthy self-image. It is impossible to overstress the value of two parents who stay together, who commit to one another, who love their children, talk to them, have fun with them, discipline them and are there for them day and night. These experiences are more precious in a child's life than a nice car, expensive holidays and having the best toys.

So that is the ideal. But what if that has not been your experience? You may have had parents who were constantly rowing and fighting. Your mum may have criticised you and put you down in front of others. Your dad may have been absent. Some parents will have created such high standards for their children that many will have a huge fear of failure and live with a sense of not being good enough. Good grades =

pleasure and praise. Failure = anger and rejection. Competition and comparisons may exist among siblings, and in this environment feelings of worthlessness may arise.

These are just a few of the harsh atmospheres that girls are growing up in today. Unfortunately this is just the tip of the iceberg. Many more suffer from the bitter effects of divorce, bereavement, alcoholism, abuse and violence. If you grew up in a home where you felt unsafe, unloved or unwanted, this will have a strong and negative effect on how you relate to others.

Personally my upbringing was a violent and rocky one. I have experienced difficulties and pain with each member of my family which made me think that if my own family couldn't love me why would anyone else? If even they rejected me then I must be awful. This belief affected so many areas of my life, including my ability to make friends and feel secure in relationships. I thought that if my parents were to divorce it would be a dream come true rather than a nightmare. However, when it did actually happen, feelings of grief and the pain of having to choose between them caused me deep agony. My home was where I was hurt, but that's not how God intended it to be. Home should be where we receive lots of love and encouragement. If, like me, this was not your experience, you may have a negative picture of yourself. Without God's affirmation you will continue to feel unsure about who you are and what you can achieve. Unless you are helped to receive healing and hear God's truth, low self-esteem can lead on to all sorts of things, including attention-seeking, insecurity, clinginess, lying, anorexia, depression, self-harm, addiction and a loveless void which leads many young girls to use their sexuality as a way to gain love and attention.

BIG SISTA: *Mary Pytches*

Five words changed my life for ever!

As long as I can remember, I had a private identity tag which had put limitations on me. I was one of those happy 'mistakes' born after my mother had finished, so she thought, with having babies. Although I was loved by my family, I had always felt like an inconvenience, until I read these five words: 'Therefore as God's chosen people . . .' (Colossians 3:12). Suddenly it dawned on me – I may have been a mistake as far as my parents were concerned, but not to God. He had planned and purposed for me to be born . . .

> I can still choose to live out of the old identity if I like, but from that day I had been given an alternative and one that I planned to stick with!

Your self-worth under the microscope

Take a look at the following questions.

1. Do you find it hard to receive a compliment?
2. Do you regularly compare yourself to others?
3. Do you become easily jealous of others?
4. Is there more than one thing you wish you could change about your body?
5. Are you continually putting yourself down?

If you answered 'yes' to more than one of these questions it is likely that you have a negative picture of yourself and are suffering from low self-esteem. How can you feel good about yourself again? Where should your sense of worth come from?

The world says, 'Do you make the grade?'

The queues build up for the latest reality TV show.

Girls practise for ages and shop for ever to achieve the perfect look. They give it all they've got and proudly show off what they believe is their God-given talent. But the judges aren't impressed. 'Sorry, you're too fat,' they say. 'Who told you that you could sing? If I were you, I'd have stayed in bed, love.'

Nice! Scrutinised, ripped to shreds, put down and rejected. Your five minutes of fame are over. Programmes like these have us glued to our sets. Three executives sit in judgement. The rest of us sit back and relax. We have become obsessed with finding the winners and losing the wannabes.

Fame is seductive and we can't deny that we've all wanted it at some point. From the age of three I was singing into my hairbrush and performing in front of my mirror. I was in bands and singing regularly from the age of 14, then at 18 I had my first showcase. An A & R man from a minor record company came to hear us play. At the end of our set he sat down with the manager and went through why we wouldn't make it. To start with he said I needed to lose at least a couple of stone and that I wasn't pretty enough. The others got a similar pasting and we went home, via the kebab shop, pretty depressed! To be told my dream was over because I was basically too fat and not pretty was horrible. The worst thing was that I had always thought those things about myself, but to hear a complete stranger say it too was gutting.

If the requirement for fame is being super-skinny, sexy and drop-dead gorgeous then I don't think many of us will make it on our own. Beauty in the eyes of the world is so narrow that it comes as no surprise that the door to eating disorders and low self-esteem is wide open. As we flick through our magazines the images we see are not teaching us anything good about ourselves. The girls look stunning and slim; they are great clothes-horses but the more we look at them the more we feel unsatisfied with ourselves. Someone somewhere is projecting to us that this is what we should look like. What depressing pressure.

God says, 'You are good enough!'

As Christians we have a refreshing alternative. When we follow God we have the option to be content with who we are. When we look at him and fix our eyes on him we start to think about 'good' rather than 'food'. We get our value from something we already have – a heavenly Father who loves us – not something we'll never have, like a pert bum and great boobs!

The Bible tells us we will not be scrutinised or rejected on the basis of our outward appearance: 'The Lord does not look at the things man looks at. Man looks at the outward appearance, but the Lord looks at the heart' (1 Samuel 16:7).

A new identity in Christ

(All verses taken from *The Message*)

● I made you in my image and likeness . . . When I saw you I saw that you are good. (Genesis 1:26, 31)

- I put you together in your mother's womb. You are awesomely and incredibly made. (Psalm 139:13–14)

- God's Spirit touches our spirit and confirms who we really are. (Romans 8:15)

Again and again our identity will be shaken unless we know, and can depend upon, the indestructible, unchangeable truth of who we really are in the eyes of Almighty God. As we seek to build up our identity on the truths of Scripture, we need the Holy Spirit to reveal the truth to our hearts. Have you ever heard someone say that your identity is in Christ and not known what it meant? This is a fundamental truth in our Christian lives; without taking holding of it and fully understanding it we are not complete.

Your mum may say you were an accident and you may feel you wish you hadn't been born. It is easy to feel in a sister's or friend's shadow – you may sometimes feel ugly and inadequate, asking, 'What are my giftings? Am I actually good at anything?' God can answer these questions and resolve your feelings of inadequacy. We belong to him and he loves us. We don't need to get on a downward spiral of despair. As girls of God we have Jesus to personally intervene and rebuild us by speaking the truth to us.

If you still find this hard to believe, there are practical ways to remind yourself to receive his truth. When I am ill, the doctor prescribes the right medicine to get rid of my pain. I pop my pills three times a day until I feel better and my symptoms have gone away. Similarly, if we are feeling low and insecure, we need to read the Bible till we feel better.

A while ago someone said something really awful and untrue about me. I was totally crushed, but I had to make a choice. I could have dwelled on what they said and believed it, but instead I simply took a verse from the Bible that was relevant to my situation and spoke it over and over again throughout the day until the cloud had lifted. It lifted because I believed and received God's truth. If you struggle with your self-image, for example, try putting one or two verses above your mirror so that every time you are tempted to look and feel worthless you will be reminded of what God says about you.

The Bible talks about being transformed by the renewing of your mind. If we let him, God will mould us into his image, renew our minds and restore our self-image. 'You shall know the truth and the truth shall set you free.'

I want to finish this chapter with another extract from Mary Pytches' excellent book *Who Am I?*

Nothing can change who we are in Christ, nothing can change our position in Christ, nothing can change the way our Heavenly Father sees us, or the affection He has for us. At the same time our distinctiveness is guaranteed. God knows us. Our names are written on the palms of His hands. Our tears counted. Every hair of our head is numbered. He calls us to Himself one by one and He gifts us individually. As if this was not enough we can rest in the knowledge that we are of utmost value to Almighty God. Not because of our performance or other people's opinion of us, but because we have been made in the image of God. Feeble, frail, ordinary human beings bear the imprint of the everlasting, All-powerful, One and Only God. The closer we walk with Him the more like Him we become. At the same time God has sealed our value by sending His beloved son to die in our place. How much more can a Father do to prove we are of utmost worth to Him? All this will add up to an identity which is beyond comparison and will outweigh and outshine any ordinary human construction.

Who am I then? I am a daughter, a sister, a student and a friend. I am also a precious, chosen, predestined, unique, loved and adored daughter of God.

2
The Truth about Girls and Girls (Friendship)

Research shows that loneliness is one of the biggest causes of depression in the UK. All you want on a summer's day is to throw down a towel and compare tans with your mates. Who doesn't want a friend they can squeeze into the changing room with and ask, 'Does my bum look big in this?' It's horrible to walk past the cinema and know that unless you go solo you're not going to be seeing that chick flick you so desperately want to see. Who wants to live life like that? Being on our own is boring and life becomes bland.

Girls need friends. We want to love and be loved. To laugh till we cry and to share our deepest hurts without the fear of back-stabbing and name-calling. Why is it that friendship can sometimes be like holding sand in our hands? Before long it slips between our fingers and is lost for ever. So what is the secret

'Does my bum look big in this?'

ingredient to making and maintaining friends?

The ingredient is God. The reason our relationships are failing and slipping between our fingers is because we leave him out of them. Without him it can end up all cat fights and catastrophes, but with him we can go deeper and build a friendship that becomes a blessing. Believe it or not the Bible can actually show us how to become better friends just by looking at the life of Jesus.

The facts

Jesus is qualified to teach us how to live and cope with the joys and trials of relationships. He lived on earth for 33 years. During that time he travelled hundreds of miles and met thousands of different types of people. In John 15:15 Jesus tells the disciples, 'I have called you friends.' In order to become the disciples' friend Jesus first had to make himself vulnerable; because of that he was able to experience the joy of friendship.

But it wasn't all good. During his life he faced both extremes of human relationships. He knew what it was like to be seen as the leader of the 'in crowd' and then to be mocked; everyone's best friend then the victim of a hate campaign. In both of these extreme situations Jesus was full of love and kindness. He pressed on to become the only perfect example we have of a true and faithful friend.

Like Jesus, we will experience the highs and lows of friendships. There will be times when the phone is ringing off the hook and our social diary is looking more impressive than an 'IT' girl's. There may also be times when we're pushed out of our friendship group and lied about by the people we trust. To learn to live in both situations we must look closer at the two extremes of popularity and unpopularity through the life of Jesus. How did he cope with being famous then friendless?

Friendless

Jesus ran into quarrels and fights because he stuck close to his values and stood up for what he believed. That meant he easily made enemies because he would not be swayed or seduced into changing. Whether it was making friends with the 'out crowd' or standing up for the outcast, Jesus was just not up for being 'in'!

What made him unpopular?

1. His friends were unpopular (Luke 19:1–10)

Jesus was passing through Jericho. Chinese whispers meant that soon a crowd had gathered to meet him. A little man with a big name and a bad reputation climbed a tree to get a better view of Jesus. That little man was Zacchaeus. He was a chief tax collector (our equivalent would probably be a chief traffic warden) and he was well known for giving people fines when they didn't deserve them. Just as we tut and mumble under our breath when we see a stingy traffic warden putting a ticket on a windscreen, people muttered and whispered when they saw Zacchaeus out and about with his money bag. He was extremely unpopular and yet Jesus called him down from the tree and invited himself to Zacchaeus's house for dinner. The crowd muttered in disgust, 'He has gone to be the guest of a sinner.' His choice had not pleased his fan club. However, Jesus was not out to impress; instead he saw that Zacchaeus was a man who needed God. So he reached out and showed kindness and friendship. Zacchaeus was converted and actually promised to give back four times the amount he had stolen.

It would be easy to understand why we should stay clear of the trouble-makers and the mean-minded, but if we are to follow Jesus' example then hanging out with them might not pollute us but in fact affect them and change their mean ways for ever!

2. He was different

If you don't want to stand out then put on your baseball cap and keep your head down. If you want to avoid a row, you'd better stay quiet. However, if you want to be true to who you are and what you believe, sometimes you have to lift up your head and speak out. Jesus wasn't afraid to do this – even when it made him unpopular. He refused to be a crowd-pulling, people-pleaser. Instead he chose to stick to the message of truth and hope, and the people flocked to him. He wasn't afraid to risk losing friends because of who he really was.

In the run-up to elections you see the prime minister and his rivals trek around the country like wannabes. Kissing babies, hugging grannies and patting dogs, they say what everyone wants to hear, grinning for the press and hoping they've impressed. Jesus wasn't a smooth talker on a popularity quest; he kept it simple: follow the hard truth or walk away. Love me or hate me, this is who I am. I am God.

Sometimes we can feel pressure to fit in and say

nothing, but if we have really committed our lives to God, surely he is worth speaking up for. Being different is not bad, it is bold!

3. He stood up for what he believed (John 8:3–11)

A woman was about to be stoned to death. In those days it was not an uncommon punishment – adultery was a serious crime. Jesus stepped in and stood up for her. The crowd that had gathered could easily have turned on him. He chose to risk his own life by protecting her from their judgement and her death sentence. He used his life to speak the truth and stamp on injustice.

In my class at school there was a girl called Frances. She was slightly odd-looking and she tended to make things up. She was an easy target for the bullies. They ridiculed her and excluded her. Even when I knew it was wrong, I didn't stand up for her. I was worried that if I stepped in maybe they would hate me too. She endured four years of torment and one day she had had enough. She forfeited her education and left school because she could not bear it any more. I often think about her. It was easy to do nothing, but I will always regret it. Jesus challenges us to stick up for the bullied, broken girls we see every day at school: not to back off but to stand alongside and be a friend; not to ask what we can gain, but what we can give.

Famous

Jesus had a group of twelve friends who followed him everywhere. He also drew crowds that were so large that he was once forced to get into a boat and row across the lake just to get some space.

There is nothing better than knowing you belong and are liked. Deep down we all want to be popular and be part of the in crowd. Funny, outgoing people tend to draw crowds and be popular, but what did Jesus have that made him such a crowd-puller? What made him popular?

1. He was a servant

Even though Jesus was God's Son he was a servant. Maybe that doesn't sound too ridiculous. But just imagine if Prince William was on royal duty in your area and as he was on his 'walk about' he spotted some dog poo, but instead of ignoring it, he got a pooper scooper and got rid of it! That would be a disgusting and lowly thing for a future king to do – such an act would never be carried out by royalty.

As God's Son, Jesus should have received the red carpet treatment and had servants on hand to meet his every need. Astonishingly, he came 'not to be served but to serve'. He washed the disciples' feet (as sandal-wearers they would have been covered in dirt and camel poo) and after he rose from the dead he cooked them breakfast. He put their needs ahead of his own. What can we learn from this?

I doubt your friends would appreciate you offering to wash their feet, but there are other ways of putting them first. For example, how many times have you found out that you and your mate fancy the same guy? That always seems to happen to good friends; maybe it's because they both have good taste! But it can end up ruining friendships. If you find out he likes you, don't just think 'Stuff it' and go for it. Think about how you would feel if that happened to you! Serve your friend by waiting till she is over him and then triple-checking she is cool with it. If she is over it and she's your friend, she should be cool. He might even have a nice mate you can hook her up with!

2. He was an encourager

He built his friends up and when they were worried

he spoke words of encouragement and comfort. When your friends are down or upset, instead of just saying 'There, there' or 'Give us a cuddle!' why not find a verse from the Bible to help them? Words are cool, but sometimes a bit of God's truth is just what we need to hear. Let's invest something of value into our friends.

3. He accepted them

His friends were not perfect. When you look at the twelve disciples it is easy to feel sorry for Jesus – they certainly had their flaws. Peter disowned him, Judas was a thief who eventually betrayed him, and James and John's nickname was 'Sons of Thunder' because they had such bad tempers.

If our friends are anything like us they will have their flaws too! It's not nice to be let down, especially by someone you trust, and a persistent let-down will be hard to stick by. In the Bible it talks about 'bearing with each other in love'. If we are going to be good friends, it is important we remember this verse. Friendship requires patience.

To strop or not to strop – that is the question!

When we do encounter fall-outs the Bible shows us

exactly how to resolve things and make up, not break up.

1. Resolve things as quickly as possible

'Do not let the sun go down while you are still angry' (Ephesians 4:26). When someone has hurt us, the more time we have to think about it, the deeper the hurt goes. We replay it in our heads again and again. We read between the lines all the things they didn't say, all the things we should have said. Our stomachs are churning. It hurts and it won't go away. We want revenge! We lay in bed replaying it once more: 'If only I could see her now. I'd get my own back, tell her what I really think of her. And I'm not the only one – loads of people think this too. I can't wait for tomorrow!'

The problem with stewing is that it produces more anger. 'I just need some space from you!' we say. When we get space, rather than giving us time to get over it, we have more time left to think! The more we think, the angrier we become. Oh dear, what a messy cycle!

God in his wisdom tells us that when we have been hurt we are not to let an evening pass. Night-time is dangerous. It is when the plotting is done. We are alone with our thoughts and things get nasty!

If you want to sort things out in a godly way, God says that it is to be done quickly. A stroppy text message, an emotional appeal to an answer-phone or a note passed via a friend is just not good enough. Go directly to your friend. Don't let it fester and don't let their sin cause you to sin. Sort it out today!

2. Resolve things as quietly as possible

If a fellow believer hurts you, go and tell him – work it out between the two of you. If he listens, you've made a friend. If he won't listen, take one or two others along so that the presence of witnesses will keep things honest, and try again. If he still won't listen, tell the church. If he won't listen to the church, you'll have to start over from scratch, confront him with the need for repentance, and offer again God's forgiving love. (Matthew 18:15–16, taken from *The Message*)

So here we have it in black and white! When we are tempted to run off and grass to the class about what a cow our mate is, we are stopped in our tracks by the truth. 'Work it out between the two of you' or as the NIV says, 'Keep it between the two of you.'

Proverbs 16:28 says, 'A gossip separates close

friends.' There is no need to involve anyone else. I know it is tempting and actually quite therapeutic to conduct a slag-off session, but there really is nothing worse than off-loading to your other mates without first making an effort to go to the person who's wronged you. How will they know if we don't say? A gentle confrontation can also simply highlight a misunderstanding on our part. So many times I have found that a tiny misunderstanding can spark off a huge feud.

Sometimes when we do say how we feel, our honesty can actually make the friendship stronger and help someone be a better friend.

3. How to do it

Proverbs 27:6 says, 'Wounds from a friend can be trusted.' As calmly as possible and without aggression it is best to explain clearly what it is your friend has done to hurt you and how it has made you feel. If you can, avoid making big accusing statements like 'You make me feel . . .', 'You always . . .', 'You never . . .', 'I'm not your friend any more . . .' or 'Amy's a better friend than you'll ever be!' Believe me, they won't help!

On the other hand, please don't feel bad about your

feelings either. I know people who end up apologising for the person rather than letting them take the responsibility themselves. Try starting with this: 'Abi, I want to chat with you because I'm feeling a bit hurt. Yesterday we arranged to walk home together but you didn't turn up. I waited for half an hour and when I rang your mum on my mobile she said you'd walked back with Sarah and the others. I felt upset, Abi. I waited for you for so long because we made an arrangement. I kept that arrangement and it feels like you have let me down because you had a better offer. Can you tell me what happened?'

Hopefully, if Abi is a good friend, she will be humble and say sorry, or at least explain if there was a misunderstanding. If she turns round and says, 'Naff off! I can walk home with whoever I want,' or makes an obvious excuse like 'I phoned your mobile loads but it just rang and rang', you then have every right to bring along one or two other friends to try again to sort it out.

Please bear in mind though that there is nothing worse than a group of girls ganging up on a solitary chick. If your gang are all yelling at her and accusing her it will make it even harder for her to say sorry. Stay calm and maybe just bring one friend with you whom Abi trusts, then gently explain again how she has hurt you. No matter how right you think you are, gentleness is the best response. Don't forget, you are trying to offer God's forgiving love, not hate and condemnation. If all else fails and you think it is necessary, perhaps you could ask your youth leader or an older friend to try and sort it out.

It is worth working through pain and misunderstanding if it means you have a friend at the end. It is better to be a servant and have a few really close friends than to be right at the centre of the in crowd and yet not be able to be yourself. Loneliness is a killer. Friendship is a gift.

Let's give to others what we would hope to receive. As we lean on God and ask him to help us, we will begin to supply a type of friendship that the world cannot give.

3

The Truth about Girls and Boys (Relationships)

The first time I saw him he was standing outside, talking in the rain. My heart jumped and I quickly but casually asked a friend who this guy was. She informed me his name was Matt Redman and he worked at the church we were visiting. Fortunately it wasn't long before I got to know Matt through a mutual friend and we started singing together in the worship band. As I saw more and more of Matt I realised he was not only incredibly nice to look at, he was also an amazing, kind-hearted man of God. My heart fluttered and I blushed at the thought of seeing him again, but I sadly faced up to the reality that this gorgeous specimen and I would never be an item! Not only did we live miles apart, but we were both pretty settled and content, and I could tell that Matt was not really interested in relationships. I got on with life and had no choice but to leave it with God. After two years of friendship and not being able to eat in each other's presence (I think they call it love sickness) we confessed our feelings and started going out. Eighteen months later we got married at the church where we originally met!

It's a romantic and almost perfect story. I got to meet and marry someone who loved me and was totally committed to God, and whom I adored and respected. Our relationship was above board and godly and just how I'd dreamed it would be. But this was the first time I'd ever had a relationship like that because, before meeting Matt, when it came to the opposite sex my life was full of big mistakes and horrible dramas. Like many young girls, I was a bit giddy when it came to guys! Instead of drawing diagrams in biology I would be sketching wedding dresses! I remember lying on my bed one night and putting together a very long prayer/wish list! The list contained preferred height, appearance, humour, character, career and godliness. I knew what I wanted and my standards were high.

Many of you may dream about what it would be like to meet the right one. No doubt thoughts of romance, marriage and companionship flutter through your head on a fairly regular basis. The important thing to remember is that this isn't wrong. In her book *Wait For Me*, Rebecca St James writes:

Unless he has specifically called you to singleness I believe that God has placed a dream inside each one of us. We have a desire for intimacy, for someone to know us fully and love us completely. We long to be able to share our hearts and still find acceptance. A guy longs to protect; a girl longs to be protected. And that's exactly the way God created us. When we follow his plan, there are great blessings in store.

God says:

'For I know the plans I have for you,' declares the Lord, 'plans to prosper you and not to harm you, plans to give you hope and a future. Then you will call upon me and come and pray to me, and I will listen to you. You will seek me and find me when you seek me with all your heart.' (Jeremiah 29:11–13)

So why is it that with every good intention to live the fairytale and get it right, we so often get it wrong? Well, to start with the pressure is huge; the average age that girls are having their first sexual experience is getting lower and lower each year. Research shows this is caused by children constantly reading about sex in magazines and seeing sex implied or acted out in sitcoms, films and soap operas. Many advertisements and billboards contain strong sexual undertones. Recently I was watching TV and was surprised to see an advert for a leading brand of disinfectant that used sex to sell its product. After thoroughly cleaning the floor, the nice couple looked suggestively at the bottle and then glanced at each other before rushing upstairs to the bedroom. Maybe there really are people out there with hygiene fetishes and I was just missing something! Nevertheless, it was shocking to see sex so nonchalantly used to sell a household cleaning product!

Another factor is that psychologists reckon girls

mature much earlier than boys. Dr Nick Barlow, a consultant paediatric psychologist at Leicester Royal Infirmary, said: 'At eleven, girls are leaning more towards adulthood, while for boys puberty is still a couple of years away. At this age boys don't have the same level of adolescent bonding and understanding as girls. Research shows that eleven-year-old girls talk a lot about boys – whereas boys of a similar age won't discuss girls at all.' As early as eleven girls are tackling romance, whereas boys are focusing on skateboards and practising magic tricks. The inevitable outcome of girls maturing more quickly than boys, and being exposed to sex early on, is that it feels normal to have experienced sex during adolescence and totally insane to want to wait till marriage.

But we can't afford to be wishy-washy or border-line. The Bible spells out the place for sex:

There's more to sex than mere skin on skin. Sex is as much spiritual mystery as physical fact. As written in Scripture, 'The two become one.' Since we want to become spiritually one with the Master, we must not pursue the kind of sex that avoids commitment and inti-macy, leaving us more lonely than ever – the kind of sex that can never 'become one.' There is a sense in which sexual sins are different from all others. In sexual sin we violate the sacredness of our own bodies, these bodies that were made for God-given and God-modeled love, for 'becoming one' with another. Or didn't you realize that your body is a sacred place, the place of the Holy Spirit? (1 Corinthians 6:17–19, *The Message*)

Among you there must not be even a hint of sexual immorality, or of any kind of impurity, or of greed, because these are improper for God's holy people. (Ephesians 5:3)

This means keeping it pure in our relationships and ultimately no sex before marriage. In fact even a hint is wrong. For Matt and I this answered the question of what we could touch when we were going out. We felt that anything other than holding hands and kissing was more than 'a hint'. However, for some young girls even kissing may be too much too soon. This is a good one to talk through with your youth leader or your parents. Some people think their relationship is the exception because they aren't having casual sex, but we must be humble and accept that God knows best and he designed sex for marriage. Anything outside of that is not God's will. Many of our friends and peers may have the attitude that experimenting with sex is healthy and normal, but that's not right for us as girls of God. In this enormous and hugely sensitive issue God has something of great worth to say to us and a very different message of truth and grace. Here are some verses to point you in the right direction:

- Run from anything that stimulates youthful lust. Follow anything that makes you want to do right. Pursue faith and love and peace, and enjoy the companionship of those who call on the Lord with pure hearts. (2 Timothy 2:22, NLT)

- Nothing in all creation can hide from him. Everything is naked and exposed before his eyes. This is the God to whom we must explain all that we have done. (Hebrews 4:13, NLT)

- But remember that the temptations that come into your life are no different from what others experience. And God is faithful. He will keep the temptation from becoming so strong that you can't stand up against it. When you are tempted, he will show a way out so that you will not give in to it. (1 Corinthians 10:13, NLT)

- It is God's will that you should be sanctified: that you should avoid sexual immorality; that each of you should learn to control his own body in a way that is holy and honourable, not in passionate lust like the heathen, who do not know God; and that in this matter no-one should wrong his brother or take advantage of him. The Lord will punish men for all such sins, as we have already told you and warned you. For God did not call us to be impure, but to live a holy life. (1 Thessalonians 4:3–7)

- Honor marriage, and guard the sacredness of sexual intimacy between wife and husband. God draws a firm line against casual and illicit sex. (Hebrews 13:4, *The Message*)

- No matter how deep the stain of your sins . . . I can make you as clean as freshly fallen snow. Even if you are stained as red as crimson, I can make you as white as wool. (Isaiah 1:18, NLT)

- Create in me a pure heart, O God, and renew a steadfast spirit within me. (Psalm 51:10)

I do not want this chapter to come across as a heavy Christian rule book full of 'don't do this, don't touch there' quotes. In fact I would much rather encourage girls to focus on Jesus and be committed to him. In 1 John 2:15 we read: 'Love of the world squeezes out love for the Father' (*The Message*). The more we concentrate on God, the more, I am convinced, we will become less and less distracted and enticed by worldly things. But in reality there is a real need for godly truth and wisdom.

This world shouts loudly and clearly that experimenting with lots of different partners is completely healthy, natural and normal. I want to tell you now that this is a total and absolute lie. In the Bible the devil is described as a liar. He comes to 'kill, steal and destroy' and turn something that God designed to be beautiful into something sinful and dirty. It is totally false to think we can do what we please and not be affected.

If I told my daughter that huge amounts of sugar were good for her, and if others told her the same thing, she would be sure it was true. She would also have no problem or a guilty conscience if she ate lots of it all of the time. To begin with she wouldn't know this was wrong because my lie tasted so good. How could something that tastes so good be bad for us? Sooner or later, though, the effects would be numerous: rotten teeth, diabetes, high blood pressure, heart disease, obesity.

Do you see what I'm saying? The more we look at the subject of sex and relationships and examine what is supposedly harmless, the more we see that we are living out the repercussions of a total lie. The effects are painful and sometimes disastrous: shame, insecurity, heartache, rejection, disease, adultery, unwanted pregnancy, abortion . . . the list goes on and on.

God says the place for sex is inside Christian marriage: one man and one woman for life in a loving and committed relationship. Of course this seems pathetic and laughable and very old-fashioned, but the fruit of this wisdom is a life overflowing with love, trust, security, wholeness, freedom and joy.

For the remainder of this chapter I thought I'd call on the help of the girls on the Soul Sista board. Based at Soul Survivor, Watford, Rachel, Andreana, Vicky, Ali, Bee and I meet regularly to pray and seek God for the conferences, day events and resources that Soul Sista set up and put on. They are all in their twenties, and when it comes to boys they are all in different situations: some single, others dating and one almost married. I have watched them and known them; I believe they will answer the questions with integrity, not only because they have a heart to encourage and to speak truth, but also because they live it out. I hope you are refreshed by what these girls have to say.

Dear Big Sista

Q: Is it OK to have a boyfriend?

Rachel: Yes, of course.

Ali: Yes. If one day you want a husband you need to first have a boyfriend. Dating is part of life and as long as we handle it well – honestly before God and being accountable to our friends – it can be really good for us. Also, having *a* boyfriend is different from having one boyfriend after another. If you find you can't be without one, it's time to start asking yourself some tough questions about your security and self-worth.

Q: Is it OK to have a boyfriend that isn't a Christian?

Rachel: Can I dare to rephrase the question? I would want to ask not 'Is it OK?', but 'Is it the best?' God wants the best for our lives. Going out with a non-Christian is not just an issue of values and sex before marriage, but more importantly an ability to share life together. If you love worship, wouldn't it be best to worship with him? If God were speaking to you, wouldn't it be best if you could chat to him about it? How can someone who will take such an important role in our lives not understand or share with us our first love and priority – Jesus?

Andreana: What is 'OK' and what is beneficial are two completely different things. It's 'OK' to touch the hob when it's hot, but you can avoid the pain and consequences by choosing to walk away! I wouldn't advise it.

Q: How far should you go? Why?

Ali: Do you want to see just how far you can push it, how much you can get away with? Or are you truly wanting to honour God, your boyfriend and yourself in every aspect of your relationship? The less you do together physically, the more chance you have of not stepping over the boundaries and ending up in difficult situations, and the more likely it is that you will respect each other and be able to be totally open with God about your relationship as a whole. A good relationship doesn't necessarily need to become a physical relationship.

Rachel: I would say kissing. I know it sounds boring,

but sex (so people tell me!) is an incredible thing and it should be treasured and not treated lightly. When boundaries are broken it is far harder to keep them again. The further you go, the harder it is to stop. Keep yourself as pure as you can.

Q: I am a Christian and I don't see why it is wrong for me to sleep with my boyfriend. We are going to get married, so what is the big deal?

Beth: A stumbling-block for many Christians can be when two people who are in a loving and committed relationship have sex outside of marriage. To them nothing immoral or sinful is going on and it can be very offensive to suggest otherwise. The truth is that the Bible tells us this is wrong. It is important to submit all areas of our life to God, not just the bits that are easy. Sleeping together may feel OK, but we must learn that obedience and submission are all part of what it takes to be a Christian. Jesus said, 'Take up your cross and follow me.' That means when we choose to follow Christ we choose to die to what we want and think is best, and begin to count the cost. Once we stop wrestling and surrender our will to him, the rewards are sweet.

Q: Me and my mate both fancy the same guy, but I've just found out that he likes me. What should I do?

Vicky: Honesty is a really important part of friendship. Proverbs 24:26 says, 'Giving an honest answer is a sign of true friendship.' If you were to start going out with the guy and not tell your friend, that would not be an honest or caring way to treat her. Jesus says we should live fully in the light, with nothing hidden. So I would talk it over with her first and maybe pray about it together too. Then if you did start going out with the guy, your friend wouldn't hear about it second hand. I would also want to be fairly sure this guy and I had a long-term future together, as otherwise it wouldn't be worth risking hurting my mate in the process. Maybe it's better to just enjoy your friendship instead.

Rachel: It depends how strong your feelings are. Do not risk a friendship for something shallow. However, I don't think that should rule out the possibility of a relationship. 'Be devoted to one another in brotherly [sisterly] love. Honour one another above yourselves' (Romans 12:10). Try to honour your friend whatever happens. Be honest with her. Ensure you talk to her first and don't let her find out what could be devastating news through someone else. Lastly, if you do end up going out, don't flaunt it in front of her – be sensitive, be sisterly!

Q: My best friend has started seeing a guy and totally dropped me. I am really hurt. She has also started to change and not come to church as much. Should I say something or just move on?

Beth: Hopefully as best mates you will want to see your friend be happy and in God's will. Sometimes being in God's will means things change. No one likes change; we can experience feelings of overwhelming insecurity and jealousy when situations like these arise. Ask God to give you a peace about it and see what happens. I wouldn't advise dropping her – that means you will both lose out on something precious. You may need to just accept her relationship and try to get to know her boyfriend without feeling threatened. However, if you genuinely feel that you are being treated unfairly, why not gently chat with your mate? If she is unresponsive, keep praying and maybe ask your youth leader for advice. In reality this guy may not be bringing out the best in her, and as her friend you need wisdom to know when to say something and when to just pray. In either of these situations I think that if you sincerely want the best for your friend, you will do the right thing.

Q: *Is it wrong that all my best mates are boys?*

Vicky: When I was growing up, most of my friends were boys. I found it OK, although when we got close there were often complications over whether one of us wanted to be more than friends. Having some good girlfriends means you can have close friendships without that complication! There are also some things it might not be appropriate to discuss with boys, so girls could help you there. The Bible encourages us to 'pursue righteousness, faith, love and peace, along with those who call on the Lord out of a pure heart' (2 Timothy 2:22). So purity and a desire to follow God are great qualities to look for in a friend. Their heart and attitude are more important than their gender. But overall I would recommend a balance of male and female friends.

Ali: The question I would ask is, 'Why are all your best mates boys?' Is it that you are the only girl in your youth group, or is it that you aren't comfortable around other girls? I think the ideal is to have a mix of male and female friends. They are good for us in different ways and one without the other means we miss out.

Andreana: I have many really great friends that are guys, but it is only girls that can truly relate to the struggles and experiences I have as a girl. I think so long as there is a healthy balance in your relationships it is fantastic to have both. I might also suggest finding older girls or women to be in your life too. There really is something to be said for people that have already lived this segment in life.

Q: All my friends have boyfriends and I don't. Is it wrong to hate being single?

Ali: Jesus came that we would have life and have it to the full (John 10:10). Therefore he wants us to enjoy life. Sometimes this is easier said than done, and if you hate being single it's no good pretending you don't. Let's be honest; as you get older there are times when being single is hard. As someone who has been single for a long (and I mean *long*) time, I believe that not only does God want us to enjoy this stage of our lives for however long it may last, but also that it is possible to come to a place of being able to say, just as Paul does in Philippians 4:11, 'I have learned to be content whatever the circumstances.' This isn't always easy, but here are my top tips:

1. Ask God to help you be content and enjoy being single. God says that if we ask we will receive (Matthew 7:7) and he is more than willing and able to help you.

2. Make a choice not to wallow in your misery or allow yourself to get pulled into a pity party with your friends. Pick one or two close friends with whom you can be honest and pray, but also give them permission to shut you up when you moan too much (and we all do that).

3. Choose instead to concentrate on all the freedom you have as a single person. It always seems that the grass is greener on the other side. One day you won't be single and you'll never get this time back with your girly friends.

Rachel: Singleness is a natural stage in every life's journey and should be embraced as a gift from God. There is a freedom in singleness. 'An unmarried woman . . . is concerned about the Lord's affairs: Her aim is to be devoted to the Lord in both body and spirit. But a married woman is concerned about the affairs of this world – how she can please her husband' (1 Corinthians 7:34). Let's make it our aim to be girls devoted to God in body and spirit. Grab hold of every day God gives and live it wholeheartedly. Don't waste years waiting for life to start when you have a boyfriend. God has plans for you now.

There is pressure everywhere. Fashions come and go, but when you flick through your glossy magazines it seems the ultimate fashion accessory is a boyfriend. I just want to encourage you that there really is no rush. In Song of Songs 3:5 it says, 'Do not arouse or awaken love until it so desires.' Boys are great friends and a good laugh, but we never seem to be allowed to simply enjoy their friendship without someone stirring or whispering and trying to force people together. There are those who would say, 'Don't have boyfriends,' and though ultimately trying to honour God and stay pure, this approach can appear legalistic. I would say don't try and rebel the other way either and become involved in things that you later regret. Enjoy your youth and the freedom of being single. Also enjoy just hanging out in groups and getting to know both boys and girls in an open and relaxed environment rather than an exclusive and heavy way. Honour God and seek him, and at the proper time you will enjoy this gift. There is a time for everything, and everything is beautiful in its time.

4

The Truth about Shining (Evangelism)

As we learn more about our true identity in Christ, we grow in confidence and security. But this new identity is not simply a comfort blanket – a cosy truth we can snuggle up to and feel comfortable and warm. Yes, of course our healing and wholeness is for us, but it is not exclusively for us! God has told us we're to be the light of the world. Jesus came and lived as a man on the earth for 33 years. He taught the saints and preached to the sinners. After his death and resurrection Jesus gathered the twelve disciples and commissioned them by saying two significant things: 'Go and make disciples of all nations' and 'I am with you always, to the very end of the age' (Matthew 28:19). Like the eldest child joining the family business we have become junior partners in the firm. Jesus says to us, 'Go and do what I have been doing. That is your job description here on earth.' He also says, 'I am with you always by my Holy Spirit and I live in you. Wherever you go I am there.'

Jesus will not be visiting your school, appearing in the flesh to perform miracles and stand up for the broken. Neither will he go on a *Pop Idol* style tour of the UK to tell people the good news about God or the reality of heaven and hell. Instead he says, 'You are the light of the world.' The only way people will meet Jesus face to face and in the flesh is through you! He calls us to be his hands – reaching out to the lost; loving, comforting, giving and sharing; holding out his forgiveness, compassion and grace. He calls us to be his feet, taking the good news to people who don't know him. For some this will even involve travelling to new places and taking the message to the nations. Above all we are to have his heart, the sort of compassion that moves us to act; loving extravagantly and showing mercy – a forgiving love that covers over a multitude of sins.

What's your flavour?

> Let me tell you why you are here. You're here to be salt-seasoning that brings out the God-flavors of this earth. If you lose your saltiness, how will people taste godliness? (Matthew 5:13, *The Message*)

When you hang out with people you catch their flavour. They leave behind a certain taste – sometimes bitter or sour. We are called to leave a God flavour behind. The Bible describes this flavour as 'saltiness'. A meal without salt is bland and tasteless. A little seasoning brings out the rest of the flavours and makes a delicious meal. When people hang out with us they should be able to taste what God is like. If we are half-hearted, weak and ashamed of our faith, how will people hear about him? If we are screwed up, unkind or promiscuous, why will people want to meet our Saviour? If we are just like everyone else, how will they taste the difference? Christianity will not seem attractive – it will be a total turn off, and if you're not careful, before long you will have lost your God flavour. Swearing, smoking and messing about with sexual stuff are all ways of saying with your life, 'I'm not with you, God. I'm with them.' Salt needs to be salty, or what use is it?

> You are the light of the world. A city on a hill cannot be hidden. Neither do people light a lamp and put it under a bowl. Instead they put it on its stand, and it gives light to everyone in the house. In the same way, let your light shine before men, that they may see your good deeds and praise your Father in heaven. (Matthew 5:14–15)

Our faith can easily become our little secret – something we keep to ourselves and only dabble in at the weekend. It is surprising to think that many girls' friends have no idea they go to church, let alone that they are Christians. This verse is saying that we should stand up and be proud, 'Let your light shine before men'. If there is darkness and you happen to have a light, you don't hide it, you share it! You don't tuck it away and try to keep it for yourself.

A friend of mine said her most embarrassing moment was when her mum came to her school to give out Bibles. The game was up, her cover had been blown. Her friends started asking if she was a

Christian too, like her mum. On the one hand she had been happy to go to church, but she also wanted that part of her life to be very separate from the life she had at school with her friends. Her embarrassment drove her to get as far away from the truth as she could. She returned some years later, regretting the wasted years spent 'hiding her lamp under a bowl'. To continue in the Christian faith we need to take these verses and learn three things:

1. Be colourful

Because God is in us we should be vibrant and colourful, not dull and bland. So many people live with the idea that Christians are boring, dull, lifeless and sad. No way! We need to show them Christ in the flesh, vibrant and full of life. We have his life in us.

2. Be confident

It's easy to feel ashamed and afraid. Being different sometimes means we'll get attention, but God can also give us boldness. God is on your side, with you and for you. You have nothing to be ashamed of, and no reason to deny who you are and what you believe.

3. Be consistent

Because of your faith, people will be watching you. They will look at you to find out what God is like. If your words are not backed up by your actions, you will not only appear hypocritical but you'll confuse people's view of God.

So how do we do it and where should we start? Clambering up on the nearest table and declaring 'Jesus is Lord' is not the best evangelistic approach. Instead of shouting it out, why not first live it out? It's not always what you say you believe, but what you do because you believe that makes the biggest impact. As others look at your life and see a difference in you, they'll be sure to ask questions and want answers. As St Francis of Assisi said, 'Preach the gospel at all times, and if necessary use words.'

Question time

As a schools worker I've been involved in many classroom debates. I have witnessed many aggressive questions and equally aggressive answers. I think the best approach is a gentle one. Although many times I've been attacked for my beliefs, it doesn't help to be defensive. The 'I'm right and you're wrong' approach won't convert anyone! A verse from the Bible that's always helped me is Proverbs 15:1: 'A gentle answer turns away wrath.' If things start to get heated, it's best to stress that this is what *you* believe and you are not forcing it on anyone else. Too often we appear arrogant, telling people they need Jesus before they have said they want him!

However, once the questions start coming, if we're caught off guard it can be quite overwhelming. It's easy to get tongue-tied and end up saying something too strong, or worse inaccurate. When I first started doing schools work I took an assembly and started to answer a question about where Jesus would hang out if he were alive today. Without thinking through the answer, I blurted out, 'Jesus would be with the prostitutes.' The entire school hall – 500 pupils and their teachers – erupted with laughter. What I had meant to say was that he'd be with the social outcasts and the needy, but what actually came out made Jesus sound like a dirty old man. I tried to explain what I meant, but no one heard me because they were laughing so much! I don't think I did the Christian faith any favours that day!

For seven years I worked as an evangelist in schools. During this time I travelled throughout the UK with four different Christian organisations and spoke to thousands of young people aged between 11 and 18 during lessons and assemblies. Wherever I went young people seemed to ask the same questions. Just in case your mates are asking you the same things today, I have included a list featuring those questions and the answers we gave. They are only a rough guideline, but I hope they'll help should you ever find yourself on the spot and lost for words.

1. What is a Christian?

A Christian is someone who believes in God. The earth didn't begin with a random big bang, nor did we evolve from monkeys. We believe that everything started with God. The story about this is in a book in the Bible called Genesis. As Christians we live our lives by what the Bible says. We find out from the Bible that God sent his Son Jesus to the earth. We do not need to argue his existence – historians have already proved that. In fact there is more historical evidence to prove Jesus' existence than Julius Caesar's. So the argument is not *if* he existed but whether he was who he said he was. He claimed he was God's

Son. As Christians we have weighed up the evidence and put our beliefs and the Bible to the test, and found him to be real.

2. *Do you* **have** *to go to church?*

If someone were a real fan of Man United they would make sure they were at all the matches. They wouldn't have to be dragged off to Old Trafford kicking and screaming. They'd happily go along because they love their team. It is the same for us. Because we love Jesus and we want to know more about him, we go along to church. We don't *have* to go; we *want* to be there.

3. *What happens at church? Is it boring?*

Normally there is some singing. We call that bit the 'worship'. What sort of music there is depends on what sort of church you go to. Some churches have DJs and dancers during the worship, while others use a more traditional style, like organ music and a choir. Where I go to church there is a really funky band with singers and quite modern music. We sing upbeat songs rather than hymns. There is a bit of praying and often someone will read a verse from the Bible. After the worship there is a talk about God. This part is helpful as it can sometimes relate to stuff we go through at school, or it can teach us a bit more about Jesus and the Bible. When it's all over, we hang around and have a drink and a chat with our mates. Because I'm totally into God I don't find it boring.

4. Why do you believe in God if you've never seen him?

Well, I've never seen the wind, but when trees blow and leaves fall I know the wind exists because I've seen the effects it has. I haven't seen electricity either, but again I know it exists when I turn the TV or the lights on. I may not have actually seen God, but I've seen the effects in my life through prayer, the Bible and unexplainable things like healing (people getting better without doctors or medicine).

5. How do you know it's true?

(a) Simple trust.   The most basic explanation is that I have put it to the test and I have found it to be true. How will someone who isn't a Christian know if Christianity really works unless they put it to the test themselves? The Bible says bold things like, 'Ask and it shall be given to you.' We can find out if this is true by putting it to the test. For example, someone needs a job, they read the verse and then pray, 'God, please help me find a job near where I live. I trust you to do this because your word says, "Ask and it shall be given to you."' And what happens? They find a job within walking distance. Of course, sometimes God answers our prayers in unexpected ways because he knows better than we do what we *really* need.

Another example: I'm feeling low and alone. Despondent, I pick up a Bible and my eyes fall on the verse 'The Lord is close to the broken hearted'. I pray, 'Lord, thank you for telling me you are close to me; please help me to feel your love too.' I am interrupted by a knock at the door! A good friend is passing by and feels she should tell me that God loves me! She comes in for a cup of tea. Not only do I feel totally encouraged, I am not lonely any more!

God shows himself to be real and true time and time again. Pass it off as coincidence if you like, but each of these examples is a real testimony to me in my life that he is alive!

(b) Deep faith. There are some things in my life that I don't understand. In each situation I need to choose to have faith. Even if I still don't understand, and the future is looking bleak, I know God is in control and he will take care of me. Many times we see only half

the picture. It is easy for panic and frustration to set in. Faith says, 'I believe that God is for me and that he sees the whole picture.' Therefore faith enables us to wait patiently. As the Bible says, 'My times are in your hands' (Psalm 31:15). We know he is looking after us, our helper and defender. 'My thoughts are not your thoughts . . . my ways [are] higher than your ways' (Isaiah 55:8–9). In this verse from Isaiah God is gently reminding us that we see things in part – just a small and limited perspective – but God sees the whole thing and is working in ways we don't see or understand.

6. If there is a God, why do bad things happen?

When God made us he decided humans with free wills were much better than robots that did what they were told without a choice! There are two responses with free will. One is obedience, the other rebellion. We can choose either to love him and follow him or to turn away from him and sin. Sometimes we think we know better than God. He allows each of us this choice, and this gives some explanation as to why much of the world is in chaos. The whole of creation is on a course for destruction.

Society doesn't want anything to do with God until

it all goes wrong. Then God gets the blame. Disasters, massacres, murders and wars are horrific acts of violence and rebellion. As Christians we can pray against things like these and ask God in his mercy to intervene.

7. Does God forgive murderers?

The Bible teaches us that 'all have sinned and fall short of the glory of God' (Romans 3:23). We all sin and deserve punishment. Through Jesus' death on the cross we can experience the gift of forgiveness. If we truly repent (recognise our sin and say sorry), we can be forgiven. This goes for everyone, including murderers, bullies and thieves.

8. If I don't believe in God does that mean I'm going to hell?

The Bible tells us that everyone will be judged. The Bible talks a lot about heaven and hell. As Christians we believe that both of these places exist.

What is heaven? Heaven is eternity with God. God is good and heaven is all the amazing things about God under one roof: eternal peace and joy, and no more sadness or suffering. What is hell? Hell is eternity without God. Hell is everything God detests.

There is evil, greed, sickness, sorrow and suffering there.

It isn't a case of goody-goodies go to heaven and murderers go to hell. Anyone who chooses to believe receives a place in heaven. For something so huge it seems so simple. By accepting Jesus, repenting and turning from our old lives to follow him we can go from hell to heaven. What an amazing destiny!

9. Does being a Christian mean that you can't drink or have sex?

Although drinking in moderation is acceptable for adults in most Christian circles (after all, Jesus turned water into wine at a wedding, so he can't be that against it!), drinking to excess is wrong. It leads to all sorts of things: loss of judgement, loss of inhibitions and self-control, and a lot of unwise, even dangerous, behaviour. In extreme cases an addiction is formed.

In all this we believe God knows what is best for us. If sex outside of marriage is good for us, why are the repercussions so bad? Hurt, rejection, sexual diseases, unwanted and teenage pregnancies and worst of all abortion can all result from our carelessness. It's not just about the bad effects it can have on us; it's about trying to be obedient to God. Because we have chosen to follow him we choose to follow his ways too. Even if that seems inconvenient or undesirable at times, that's part of a Christian's way of trying to honour God in their life.

10. Isn't Christianity just a load of rules and regulations?

We all need rules. Without them we would just do what we wanted and end up suffering the consequences. God isn't bossy and boring; he is a wise and loving Father who knows what is best for us. When we see the guidelines God gives us, we can be resentful and say, 'Who are you to tell me what I can and can't do? I want to go out with that guy, sleep with him, drink and take drugs, and no one is going to stop me.' Or our attitude can be one of love and obedience: 'I accept God's ways are better than my ways, and I choose to follow him and not myself. I will not rebel or fight against my God. I love God, and because I also trust him 100 per cent, I know he has shown me the best way to live my life, and I am grateful.'

But being a Christian is not just about having the 'right' answers. The biggest challenge now is to live your life and not lose your saltiness. Christianity isn't about staying at home and trying to be 'saintly'. It is OK to go out with your friends, but make sure you take your God flavour with you. Let them taste it by consistently preaching the gospel with your life. When they see you making a difference, I guarantee they will ask questions. And when they do, be ready to answer, honestly and boldly.

Remember God is with you on your journey. Sometimes God's power is most evident in our weakest and most vulnerable moments. Many times I have stood in front of a class of bored and annoyed-looking 15-year-olds and thought, 'I just can't do this.' As I've stood up, the fear is apparent – red cheeks, sweaty palms and muddled words. There have been some horrible moments: I have been shouted at, laughed at and even spat on. But throughout all of the weakness and embarrassment, I've experienced the overwhelming privilege of telling people about Jesus. I have personally had the opportunity to hear their struggles and answer some of their questions. Most amazing of all, I have witnessed hundreds make a first-time commitment to God. Lost and confused, hurting and alone, they find their Saviour and go from hell to heaven. That is what our lives are all about!

We have the privilege of knowing him. Someone

somewhere showed us what he was like, and since then our life and our destiny have been changed for ever. We have that same privilege: to show others what he is like and lead them to the cross. It isn't a shameful duty – it is an inherited calling.

God is with us, helping us and changing us to be salty 'light-bearers'. I wouldn't want to be anything else!

5
The Truth about Forgiveness (Part 1)

The amazing change that takes place when we become Christians starts right here with the subject of forgiveness. The truth is, we possess something we did not earn, could not buy and cannot even get our heads round.

In Luke 7:36–50 Jesus had been invited over to the home of a local prestigious leader, a Pharisee. During dinner the host had planned to get time alone with Jesus so he could suss out exactly what he was up to. But right in the middle of the evening's proceedings an uninvited woman burst in. Snivelling and bawling, she fell at the feet of Jesus. Yes, it was every man's worst nightmare – a crying woman!

Her background was not an impressive one. We believe this woman was either a prostitute or someone who was known for some sort of sexual sin, possibly adultery. To everyone else at the dinner table it was obvious who she was and what should be done with her. Eyebrows were raised as the supposed 'God-send' did nothing. The Pharisee looked down his nose and cast his judgement: the case was closed – Jesus was a fraud. After all, if he was such a wise prophet, he would have known what sort of woman was sitting at his feet. Any respectable leader would have had her thrown out onto the street.

Of course Jesus knew who this woman was, and so did she. She had earned a reputation that she could not shed. Disgraced and disliked, a hopeless case, she had found Jesus. His message of forgiveness and freedom had overwhelmed her and given her hope. To be told she was clean was something she never thought would happen. To others, like the Pharisee, she would always be a dirty rotten disgrace. Yet Jesus had told her, 'Your sins are washed away.' Now a new life had begun.

No doubt she had wept over the cruel judgements that her past had earned her. But now in this Pharisee's front room, she'd finally tracked Jesus down and was overwhelmed with thanks. She brought an alabaster jar of perfume (rumoured to be worth a year's wages) and poured it over his feet. And there she sat, without shame, weeping tears of relief, gratitude and awe. Who could have known, apart from herself and Jesus, what was actually going on? To all around, this just seemed like an immoral display of lust and emotion. But this was her worship. She loved her Lord and she'd come to bow down and simply say thank you.

Sometimes when people who aren't Christians visit lively churches they miss what is actually going on. They frown at the crazy songs. They smirk at all the arms waving in the air and the funny hopping up and down that we like to call 'dancing'! To them it just seems meaningless and over the top. For us it means everything. Forgiven and thankful, we don't care what it looks like or what people think. We are on a mission to give God praise.

A few years ago I was at a well-known Christian conference with my husband when I bumped into a lady from my old church. I hadn't seen her for some years and as I began to introduce Matt she blurted out, 'I bet Beth hasn't told you what she used to be like. I've got so many stories!' On and on she went with story after story, laughing and thinking Matt must be enjoying these tales. I stood there biting my lip, trying not to cry. It hurt so much.

When I see people like this from my old school or youth group days, I am tempted to hang my head in shame. The things I did as a teenager seemed to have gained me a reputation that, even in my 20s, I could not shed. Unfortunately, in their minds, I will always be that person, and the enemy would love to persuade me to live in that shame. Fortunately, I asked God for forgiveness and I have been forgiven and changed. Amazingly, I am no longer that person, so I don't have to live under that judgement or shame. The immature mistakes, the deliberate wilful acts and the plain rebellion were all taken away from me when I became a Christian. I am free to be at peace with my past. 'If anyone is in Christ, they are a new creation; the old has gone, the new has come!' (2 Corinthians 5:17).

A new day

I was brought up to go to church and believe in God. But even though I knew it was true – and I'd witnessed it to be real – I chose to do my own thing. I enjoyed taking part in church, singing and socialising, but my own life was far from what I'd heard preached at youth group and the words I happily sung along with at church. I was probably every youth leader's worst nightmare!

There were some reasons for the way I lived outside of church: pain, insecurity, family problems and peer pressure. But, at the end of the day, I'd never really given myself 100 per cent to God. I hadn't experienced the amazing things that happen when you turn your back on the old life and you live for him and he lives in you. I did not understand the power of prayer or the incredible way that the Bible can bring light, truth and comfort to so many different situations. When I really turned around and stopped doing things I knew were wrong, I experienced the amazing sense of his forgiveness, and a fresh start. This is when life for me really began.

It says in John 10:10 that Jesus has come that we may have life, and have it to the full. When we're half-hearted about him (or, as Jesus put it, 'lukewarm') we're stopping ourselves from living in the fullness of God. We miss out on this incredible freedom, friendship and forgiveness.

Things changed for me when I went on a Christian holiday. No one there would have known my real state. At the start of the holiday even I would have considered myself a Christian. But the more time I spent with people who were really on fire for God, the more I realised there was a massive difference between my Christianity and theirs. Every evening someone would preach, and each time I felt more and more gripped by the truth, convicted that I'd never really chosen to follow God with a whole heart. I'd joined a fantastic social group based on something I truly believed in, but I chose to have the best (or rather worst) of both worlds by trying to be a bit of both. I did what I pleased outside of church. I smoked and regularly got very drunk, and I also messed around with guys. As you can imagine, this gave me quite a reputation around the church and the classroom.

God in his grace has taken those things and wiped them out of my life. Like the money lender (in the story from Luke 7) he cancelled my debts and wiped them out. So at the age of 18 I had a fantastic clean slate – a brilliant plain page in front of me. And all those labels ('liar', 'tart', 'loser', 'hopeless case') were completely erased! It does not mean those things never happened, and it doesn't even mean that I haven't suffered any of the consequences of my sin. I deeply regret the wasted years I spent drinking and throwing myself at boy after boy. I am gutted that when I was at school I didn't stand up for God. But more than anything, I'm humbled that my God still received me. He gave his beloved Son, Jesus, who in dying on the cross took all my many sins and buried them with him. Then he rose again, and so did my new life in him. Don't waste your youth on worthless sin – let God be glorified today!

Refreshing truth

- As for you, you were dead in your transgressions and sins, in which you used to live when you followed the ways of this world and of the ruler of the kingdom of the air. (Ephesians 2:1–2)

- But because of his great love for us, God, who is rich in mercy, made us alive with Christ even when we were dead in transgressions – it is by grace you have been saved. (Ephesians 2:4–5)

- In him we have redemption through his blood, the forgiveness of sins, in accordance with the riches of God's grace that he lavished on us with all wisdom and understanding. (Ephesians 1:7–8)

- As far as the east is from the west, so far has he removed our transgressions from us. (Psalm 103:12)

So what does this mean for you? It means that God does not want you to live your life beating yourself round the head, feeling ashamed and continually saying sorry for things he's already forgiven. The truth is that once we've said sorry and received this forgiveness, God then says, 'I remember your sins no more.'

Just as the east and the west will never meet, so our past sins will never be joined to us again. There is now a choice to make. We can believe a lie and dwell on the past, or we can choose to be like the woman in Luke 7 who received forgiveness from God and fell at the feet of Jesus and worshipped. When it says in

Romans that 'his grace is sufficient for you', it means it is enough for you and your life – whatever you've done. As a forgiven person, you are now free. Choose to receive this truth and then enjoy living in the wonder of it.

6

The Truth about Forgiveness (Part 2)

An envelope dropped on the mat. It was for me. I was only 18 and not used to receiving my own post. I looked inside and could not believe it. 'MUM! Guess what! I've won a competition!' In big bold letters it informed me that I was now £20,000 richer! At this point excitement prevented me from realising that somehow I'd won a competition I had never actually entered! As naïve as it must sound, I believed that just as the letter stated I'd been 'selected at random' and could now put my feet up and live off my undeserved earnings. Of course I soon sobered up when I read the very, very small print. It stated that I would be required to send a small £100 administration fee to process my huge cheque. Apparently this was normal and should be done as soon as possible or my winnings would be handed over to someone else. Commonsense prevailed. I realised that the only prize I had won was 'Bimbo of the Year'. There was no £20,000 win. Someone was just trying to make a few quid, and I'd been taken for a ride!

You'd think I wouldn't be so stupid again, but only last year Matt and I received a mysterious letter. It was from a solicitor in Nigeria. Amazingly Matt was the sole beneficiary in the will of a minister who had recently died. Apparently this man had been at a meeting where Matt had led some worship. Despite the fact he had his own family, he'd changed his will and decided Matt should have all his money. We had been tracked down and informed of his sad and sudden death.

I'm sure you're thinking this was an obvious set up, but Matt and I had been experiencing some money problems and I assured my husband this was our answered prayer! After much persuasion from me,

Matt decided to email the solicitor and find out a bit more about it. To our surprise, the reply stated that this was all legitimate and that we had been left nearly a million dollars. What a blessing!

Matt decided we should give it away or use it for the ministry. I decided we would have homes in London, Milan and Paris! Unfortunately, neither of these dreams came to pass. Soon after this we were in contact with Scotland Yard – and discovered that we'd almost been taken for a huge fraudulent ride!

So where's the catch?

When we hear about God's grace it is easy to think there must be a catch. After all, you don't get something for nothing in this world. You have to buy one to get one free, so it's not free after all, is it? But there really is no catch when it comes to grace. It's a free gift. Here's how one worship song describes it:

> The grace of God upon my life
> Is not dependent upon me,
> On what I have done
> Or deserved,
> But a gift of mercy from God,

Which has been given unto me
Because of His love,
His love for me.

It is unending, unfailing,
Unlimited, unmerited,
The grace of God given unto me.

Judy Pruett © 1990 Kingway's Thankyou Music.
Used by permission.

It has fallen into your lap with your name on it, because that is how God has decided it shall be. It is up to you what you do with it.

We can easily lead ourselves to believe that as Christians we *have* to be good and kind. We can feel it is our duty to be forgiving. The truth is that the Bible says you don't *have* to do anything: 'If you are led by the Spirit, you are not under law' (Galatians 5:18).

However, God does give some guidelines: 'Freely you have received, freely give' (Matthew 10:8). In the same way that we have freely and gladly received the gift of God's forgiveness, we are encouraged to freely give it away to others.

This is explained in more detail in Matthew

18:21–35 (NLT). Peter, one of the disciples, is fed up. He has been hurt by the same person yet again. He is now coming to the end of his tether and starting to think that maybe they don't deserve any more chances. So Peter comes to Jesus and asks him, 'Lord, how often should I forgive someone who sins against me? Seven times?' 'No!' Jesus replied. 'Seventy times seven!'

I think Peter probably thought that to forgive someone seven times was being quite gracious. Jesus responds by saying that 490 is a more acceptable number of times!

This is obviously not a story about maths or the times table. Jesus is making the point that we need to take our 'tally chart' off the wall and stop counting and just keep forgiving. But we stamp our feet and whine like a two-year-old, 'Why should I?!' Because that is how God has treated us:

Therefore, the kingdom of heaven is like a king who wanted to settle accounts with his servants. As he began the settlement, a man who owed him ten thousand talents was brought to him. Since he was not able to pay, the master ordered that he and his wife and his children and all that he had be sold to repay the debt. The servant fell on his knees before him. 'Be patient with me,' he begged, 'and I will pay back everything.' The servant's master took pity on him, cancelled the debt and let him go.

But when that servant went out, he found one of his fellow-servants who owed him a hundred denarii. He grabbed him and began to choke him. 'Pay back what you owe me!' he demanded.

His fellow-servant fell to his knees and begged him, 'Be patient with me, and I will pay you back.'

But he refused. Instead, he went off and had the man thrown into prison until he could pay the debt. When the other servants saw what had happened, they were greatly distressed and went and told their master everything that had happened.

Then the master called the servant in. 'You wicked servant,' he said, 'I cancelled all that debt of yours because you begged me to. Shouldn't you have had mercy on your fellow-servant just as I had on you?' In anger his master turned him over to the jailers to be tortured, until he should pay back all he owed.

This is how my heavenly Father will treat each of you unless you forgive your brother from your heart. (Matthew 18:23–30)

Reading this makes me realise what a hypocrite I have been too. Who am I to hold such a small thing against my brother or sister or friend when God has forgiven me for so much big stuff? It's easy to let little incidents of unforgiveness finish off our friendships.

One of my weaknesses is that I have a tendency to write people off. Because of my past I sometimes over-react when people hurt me. My defence mechanism is to shut them out of my life. My heart says, 'I let you in once and you hurt me, so I'm not going to let you do it to me again.' I close the door on that person with, 'It was nice knowing you. See you later!'

Not only does this sort of reaction cause a nasty shadow to hang over me because it constantly bugs me, but time and time again I have let my pride cause a small thing to ruin a great big friendship.

Here are some ways to recognise the beginnings of unforgiveness:

1. Lump in the throat

Seeing this person or hearing about them unexpect-edly can cause an immediate physical reaction. Something inside of you is saying, 'I have a problem with this person.'

2. Gossip

If someone has hurt you, the quickest way to get it off

your chest is to pass it on and gossip about them. This can cause division in friendships and can be very harmful to both parties. If there is someone you are constantly wanting to run down (and it is not just down to jealousy) you need to stop talking about them. Instead go to them honestly and gently, or if that's not appropriate just take it straight to God. But, as quickly as possible, extend a little grace and forgiveness.

3. Over-reacting

If you become easily upset and fly off the handle when a person's name is mentioned, your response shows that your feelings are having a hold over you and are causing you to be irrational.

4. Grudges

A few clumsy comments from a friend at school can easily build up and turn into a grudge. Each unforgiven slip will eventually add up to one big grudge. These destroy relationships because, as hard as you try to, you cannot enjoy a friendship when under the surface there are so many hurt feelings. Start by working out where the grudge actually started and pray it through from there.

5. Bitterness

This one is scary because to have bitterness you have allowed unforgiveness and grudges to exist for a while. The Bible talks about a 'root of bitterness' being like a small weed that spreads and gains control of a plant's solid and healthy foundations. Bitterness creeps in and before long it has killed the whole plant. Someone like this is easy to spot. Warped and whiny, they see most things in a negative light and become touchy and insecure around cheerful and positive people.

Bitterness is an easy way for the enemy to ruin an otherwise healthy Christian. But just as a good gardener knows how to get rid of a lethal weed – no matter how it has spread – God is able to free someone from the destruction bitterness brings. It is essential to get help soon.

6. Revenge

When we carry unforgiveness in our hearts, we want to see justice done, or we want to see the person who has hurt us punished. Unforgiveness, and the anger it brings, gives us power over others. When we forgive, we lose that power – we give it to God and we are free. The hard part in all this is that while we have the choice not to sin, we don't always have the same choice not to be sinned against. Very wrong things can happen to us. It is a reality that many young girls are abused, assaulted and mistreated by others – often by a family member. They find themselves having to deal with the consequences of someone else's evil, which unfairly has the potential to ruin or spoil their lives.

If this does occur, how do we get over it? We may wrestle with releasing forgiveness. After all, we did not ask for this to happen, and we certainly did not deserve it. So why should we have to forgive? Surely to forgive is letting them get away with it?

'"It is mine to avenge; I will repay," says the Lord' (Romans 12:19). 'For we must all appear before the judgement seat of Christ' (2 Corinthians 5:10). These verses show us that even if our hurts aren't resolved on this earth they will be one day. Ultimately God will do the judging and the punishing. Believing this and applying it to our situations brings peace and relief. God will win the battles for us.

His forgiveness is our resource

As you pray, know that the act of forgiveness does not condone what has been done to you. Instead you are actually choosing to put it behind you. Forgiveness says, 'I will not let this person, or their sin, dominate, control or rule me.' You are choosing to give it to Christ.

We won't always feel we have the strength or ability to forgive. If you're finding it hard to forgive someone, why not start back at the cross? Examine all that Jesus has done for you, all that he has saved you from, and how forgiven you now are. Then look again at that issue of unforgiveness. It's easier to forgive when we truly get hold of how much we have been forgiven ourselves. Many times when I have really been sinned against I have had to ask God to help me forgive. I simply cannot do it on my own. In our weakness God will help us to be merciful and enable us to release forgiveness.

If it is a very big thing, approach a trusted friend or leader and ask them to pray about it with you. The main thing is not to let unforgiveness get hold of you. In the case of abuse it is essential to find a Christian counsellor who can help you to talk and pray it through. You cannot live with this alone.

Jesus was human. He showed us that he felt things as strongly as we do. Yet so often we can think of him as a 'non-feeling' God. When bad things happen to us, it's OK to feel angry. He felt angry. He also taught us how we should respond to anger. Paul said, 'In your anger do not sin' (Ephesians 4:26). Do not let what someone else has done to you cause you to sin against someone else, and God.

God wants us to be free from the burden that unforgiveness brings – not to be bitter and angry for ever, but instead to bring our hurts to him so that he can take them. The truth is that when we forgive, whatever has been said or done to us will no longer have the same hold on us. Jesus' truth speaks into our situation, 'It is finished. Now go in peace. You are free!'

7

The Truth about Destiny

If I were to ask you what your dreams are, I wonder what you would say. Maybe you can sing, dance or act, and you long to use your gifts to tell people about Jesus. Perhaps you feel a calling to teach, train and disciple, or be a missionary and study/teach overseas. Maybe you simply long to be a wife and a mother one day. Whatever the difference in detail, the desire is the same: you have a deep longing and a far-off dream that bubbles inside and won't go away.

When I was a teenager I absolutely loved singing. In Year 10 everyone was given an interview with a lady from the careers department. She rolled her eyes when I told her I wanted to be a singer. It didn't put me off – I was determined and it was all I could think about. When I committed my life to God, my passion for singing remained, but my dream had a new focus. I wanted to use my singing to tell people about Jesus.

However, although I was confident with friends I could not speak or sing in public without going red and having panic attacks! Every day when the teacher took the register I dreaded having to call out, 'Here, Sir.' If I was picked on to answer a question in class I would look down and get a rash on my neck, which my friends fondly referred to as my 'alien neck'. Not only was I lacking in confidence, I also knew that realistically there were many other singers who were heaps better than I was. No way would I get picked instead of them. However, my desire did not go away and I decided to keep on praying. If this was God's will then he could make it happen and give me confidence.

After I properly committed my life to God, I lay on my bedroom floor trying to write a song and all I could think about was the fact that I wanted to tell young people about Jesus. I prayed that God would enable me to do this and that he would open the doors, because I didn't know any way that this could happen. Two huge answered prayers later, in a matter of only two months, I was standing up in front of hundreds of kids, talking and singing about God as an evangelist in schools. A friend of a friend had got in touch looking for a singer to join their band. They did lots of gigs and schools work and they asked my friend if they knew anyone who would fit the bill! I was astounded. I never thought God would use me. I hadn't even been able to answer my name in class, so how would I speak to a room full of school kids?

But I learned a valuable lesson about God that I want to pass on to you. God wants you to dream big dreams with him. He also wants to give you the opportunity to fulfil those dreams. The Bible says clearly, 'He will give you the desires of your heart' (Psalm 37:4). We follow a God who has given us gifts and abilities, so naturally we have a longing to use and develop those things. If you are blessed with the ability to sing, dance, act, lead worship, teach, nurture or care for others, then that blessing has come from him. We don't have to learn to live in frustration and put the things that we love on the back burner; we simply need to submit those things to him.

For example, my gifting is an entrustment – a gift God has given me to glorify him. Of course it's OK to enjoy doing the things we're called to, but the gift is never more important than the giver of the gift. We need to keep checking we're pursuing God ahead of our dreams.

Another lesson we can learn from the Bible is that we don't have to carry the burden of trying to make it happen ourselves. Revelation 3:7 says, 'What he opens no-one can shut, and what he shuts no-one can open.' This verse gives me great confidence and has proved so true in many lives. Even though we may have many practical or physical odds against us, God is able to open up opportunities and use us beyond our wildest dreams. Of course human nature says it will never happen; how on earth could it? All around you there are more popular and more talented people whose futures look much brighter than yours. If your name was thrown into a hat of people at school 'most likely to succeed', would your name be called? The chances are it would not. Worldly success is based on shallow things such as looks, wealth, popularity, status and charm, but the Bible says that a future with God is based on much deeper things.

> Brothers, think of what you were when you were called. Not many of you were wise by human standards; not many were influential; not many were of noble birth. But God chose the foolish things of the world to shame the wise; God chose the weak things of the world to shame the strong. He chose the lowly things of this world and the despised things – and the things that are not – to nullify the things that are, so that no-one may boast before him. (1 Corinthians 1:26–28)

When God chooses his workers, the one thing that matters on their CV is the state of their heart. Should we settle on the assumption that we'll be overlooked and our dreams will have to die? No way! Go to the Bible and it clearly says that God is the 'door-opener'. God has a plan for us; if his will is for us to do something, and we are faithful, be assured that he will cause it to happen.

Often disappointment and confusion come when we feel nothing is happening and we've been waiting for a long time. 'There is a time for everything, and a season for every activity under heaven' (Ecclesiastes 3:1). God's timing is often very different from ours. One of the biggest mistakes we make is trying to rush God. We may think we are ready, but only God knows the perfect time. When the season's right, be assured that he will release you to do the things that are burning inside your heart.

BIG SISTA: *Loretta Fenton*

The first time I ever felt God speaking directly to me was through the Bible. I was 14 years old and had not been a Christian for very long – a matter of months. I attended a youth event where some young Christians from America were over in the UK singing, dancing and performing drama sketches in schools and talking about their faith. The group made such an impact on me that I remember praying, 'God, this is so what I want to do with my life. If I could use my love for singing and dancing and tell others about you at the same time, that would be my dream come true.'

I went home that night and prayed to God that one day he would give me my heart's desire. Then I opened my Bible, desperate to hear from God. To my amazement, the page it opened on spoke directly to me. It was Ecclesiastes 11:9, and was titled 'Advice to Young People'. It said, 'Young people, enjoy yourselves while you are young; be happy while you are young. Do whatever your heart desires, whatever you want to do. But remember that God will judge you for everything you do.' I was amazed. I couldn't believe that God was concerned enough with me and my dreams to tell me, all but outright, to go for it!

I held on to that promise from God, delighted that he had shown me that what he puts in our hearts as dreams is often an indication of what we are called to. It came as such a wonderful revelation to me that he wants us to be happy and fulfilled. He wants to give us our heart's desires. This can really help you as a young person if you are beginning to think about what you want to do with your life.

I never forgot that verse, but it wasn't until five years later that I started to see the fruit of this promise. God amazingly sorted it out for me to attend the School of Creative Ministries. I then joined the World Wide Message Tribe and from there I was a part of pop/R&B girl band 'Shine'. I have learned through all of this that God is faithful to his word and his word is powerful and true.

What to do in the meantime

Look at the story of Joseph. He had a dream that God would use him massively. He was so excited that he couldn't keep that dream to himself. Unwisely he told his older brothers that he would rule over them one day. Not surprisingly his boasting got him thrown into a hole and sold into slavery. After many miserable years, struggling and suffering, his dream finally did come to pass. A lesson we must learn from the life of Joseph is to be humble and wait patiently.

I have one friend who used to work in a Christian recording studio, serving teas. Now she is a well-known musician. She faithfully served God in the small things for years before she finally got to do the thing she'd dreamed about. I didn't even know she could sing – she kept it so quiet!

If you feel God has given you something to do in the future, hold on and store it up in your heart. I have had many young girls come up to me and reel off the news that they are going to be the next big thing in the Christian scene! Whatever dreams you have, keep them between you and God and continue pray-ing and being faithful in the little things: serving at church, helping with the kids work, putting the chairs away – all these things are ways of serving God and showing that you are willing to wait patiently.

So what about when exciting opportunities and open doors come our way, and we've got big decisions to make? College or sixth form? University or a year out? Full-time church ministry or full time in the city? What about our dreams? When it comes to making these decisions we can be certain that if we continue to seek God he will continue to guide us. If we ask for wisdom, he will give it.

- Many are the plans in a man's heart, but it is the Lord's purpose that prevails. (Proverbs 19:21)

- In his heart a man plans his course, but the Lord determines his steps. (Proverbs 16:9)

- Trust in the Lord with all your heart and lean not on your own understanding; in all your ways acknowledge him, and he will make your paths straight. (Proverbs 3:5)

- Commit to the Lord whatever you do, and your plans will succeed. (Proverbs 16:3)

BIG SISTA: *Wendy Virgo*

I had been taught from an early age that the Bible is very important. It not only tells us what God is like, and about the history of his people, and how he wants us to live, but it is also a source of guidance to us. It helps us to make choices in our lives. Sometimes it speaks into our situation very specifically.

When I was 18, I went to college in London. I wanted to get a degree and be a teacher. In my final year, I needed to get a sense of direction. Where did God want me to go next? I wanted to go abroad, and tried applying in various places, but nothing opened up. An old friend got in touch and told me she had had a wonderful year with an overseas organisation that placed students and young people in other countries to give voluntary aid in places of deprivation. My friend had been working in a school in Malawi. This was what I wanted to do. It was adventurous and useful, and also an opportunity to spread my wings and see another part of the world.

I obtained the necessary forms and began to fill them in. When I got to the bottom of the page I realised I would need a reference. I thought my tutor would be a good person to ask, so I got up from the desk to find her. My hand was on the door knob when a thought struck me, 'She will ask me if I have prayed about this.' I knew the honest answer was 'No'. I hesitated. Perhaps I should pray first before seeing her. So I went to my bed and prayed, 'Lord, I am sorry I have assumed that this is OK with you without really seeking your will. Please will you speak to me now and help me to hear you clearly?' I opened my Bible. My eyes fell upon some verses in Psalm 32: 'I will instruct you and teach you in the way you should go; I will counsel you and watch over you. Do not be like the horse or the mule, which have no understanding and must be controlled by bit and bridle or they will not come to you' (verses 8–9). The words went like an arrow to my heart: God was saying I must not rush ahead like an uncontrolled horse, doing what I thought was a good idea. I must wait patiently and trust him to lead me. I stood up and stared at the form I had filled in. Then slowly I tore it up.

Did I ever regret that decision? No. I am so glad God spoke into my life at that point. A few weeks after that, I began to go out with Terry, the man who became my husband, and with whom I have had a very happy and fulfilling life as we have worked together for the kingdom of God.

People are generally fascinated with finding out the future. Many go in search of answers by looking into astrology, palm reading, tarot cards and many more unreliable and dodgy methods. However, there's no one on this earth who can accurately predict our future apart from God. The Bible says that our times are in his hands (Psalm 31:15). He knows what we will do with our lives – if we will marry and have children, what careers we will have and how long we'll live. He has your life mapped out before you. 'All the days ordained for me were written in your book before one of them came to be' (Psalm 139:16).

The unshakeable truth is that there is no one else like you. God has created you with gifts and abilities and a purpose to fulfil. What is that purpose and when will it be fulfilled? Only he knows, but as you continue to follow him he will teach you his ways and open the doors. I remember being around the age of eight years old when my family took me to a Christian conference called the Downs Bible Week. I went along to the children's meetings and stood on the chair singing along. Suddenly the words of a song gripped my little heart.

I have a destiny I know I shall fulfil,
I have a destiny in that city on a hill.
I have a destiny and it's not an empty wish,
For I know I was born for such a time as this.

Long before the ages You predestined me
To walk in all the works You have prepared for me.
You've given me a part to play in history,
By the power of your Spirit working mightily.

Mark Altrogge © 1986 People of Destiny Int. adm. by
Copycare, P.O. Box 77, Hailsham BN27 3EF.
Used by permission.

Being only eight years of age I didn't fully understand the words, but I did understand the basic sentiment. God had a plan for my life. I'd been 'born for such a time as this' and for the first time in my life I knew I was here for a reason. It was so exciting! Home life was hard and I slipped in and out of Christianity as I struggled with pain and heartache. When I returned to God and fully committed my life to him I was 18. Ten years before that I had felt God give me a dream. Now, ten years later, I had finally begun to walk in it.

You too have a destiny. It's not an empty wish that

must live in a file named 'disappointment'. God has planned for you to be alive today and his hand is on your life. He is for you and he has 'works prepared in advance' for you to do. It is only through him that these things will come to pass. Don't allow yourself to believe you are a waste of space or a worthless dreamer. You have a destiny. Your life is for a reason. Hang on to him and let his truth set you free, and don't ever stop dreaming big dreams for his kingdom and his glory. Amen!

8

How to Have a Quiet Time

In Psalm 119:9 the writer asks the question, 'How can the young keep their way pure?' This is something we'd all love to know. How do we do this Christianity thing successfully? The problem seems to be the same for everyone; we love God and we want to follow him, but it's hard to stay on track.

Every summer I attended a Christian family conference with my youth group. Together we experienced many deep things with God in a loving and supportive environment. One significant part of the conference was the Bible teaching, which was communicated in a simple and exciting way. I always returned home enthusiastic and fired up. By early September, once the school term had started, my vows and good intentions began to slowly slip away as real life beckoned. I found it impossible to sustain my devotion without the support and presence of my summer experience. I just didn't know where to start. I got into a downward spiral and each year by Christmas I was positively backslidden. This cycle continued until I grabbed the Bible with both hands and took hold of the answer to the psalmist's question for myself. 'How can a young woman keep her way pure?' Answer: 'By living according to your word.'

Just as we drink water to stay alive, living in God's word enables us to survive in our world. Imagine a day without drinking any water. Most likely you would experience a bad headache and a very dry mouth. Now imagine a week . . . you simply could not survive. Our bodies are designed not to go even three days without water. Spiritually, many of us are dehydrated because we're not drinking enough. There are many ways to quench a thirst like that, and one way is through reading the Bible.

Over the years I've found that the key to spiritual stability is living in God's word. Each time I pick up the Bible and live my life according to it, I fall off the spiritual rollercoaster and gain a sort of 'God momentum'. The Bible is crammed full of instruction, correction, wisdom, revelation and encouragement that enables me to feed myself rather than just rely on Christian events to keep me alive spiritually. These events then become a bonus rather than a lifeline.

> All Scripture is God-breathed and is useful for teaching,
> rebuking, correcting and training in righteousness, so
> that the [woman] of God may be thoroughly equipped
> for every good work. (2 Timothy 3:16–17)

So with renewed passion we pick up the Bible, but
where exactly do we start? It isn't a novel, so it would
be unwise to start at the beginning and expect to
reach the end by next month! It is to be taken in
stages – each of the 66 books it contains teaches us
something different.

The book of Genesis begins the story. It's the foun-
dation of all we believe. Genesis 1–11 tells us that the
eternal God created all things 'good'. We are made in
his image, for relationship and rulership over the
earth. In our freedom we rebelled against him, claim-
ing to be our own god (the Fall) and then horrible
things happened: murder (Cain and Abel), total
corruption (except for Noah and his family in the
flood), and pride reaching to heaven (the tower of
Babel). If you look closely, this book includes some
biology, astronomy, anthropology and chemistry!

But God's plan for us was never overturned.

Starting with Abraham he promised to bless a special family (the Jews) and through them bless the whole world. This set the stage for Jesus' birth almost 2,000 years later.

From Exodus to 2 Chronicles (look at the contents page of your Bible) the story line is God delivering his people from slavery in Egypt and giving them his word (the Law) and his worship (the Tabernacle and later the Temple) and taking them to his special land (the Promised Land). Along the way bad things happened, but God was faithful in preparing for the final salvation in Jesus Christ.

In the middle of the Old Testament there is a book called the Psalms, the prayer book of the Bible. It is a great thing to read a psalm each day. Here we learn how to pray, meditate, worship and be honest with God. Both individuals and groups used the psalms as prayers for private devotions and public praise, and we can do the same today.

After Psalms comes the book of Proverbs – a brilliant book full of short and snappy bits of wisdom from a king called Solomon. Here's an example: 'A fool's mouth is his undoing, and his lips are a snare to his soul' (Proverbs 18:7). This is a great verse to pull us up when we've been gossiping or saying too much!

The final big section of the Old Testament is the prophets. These people are God's mouthpieces. They speak his words of love and warning into our lives and predict much of the future fulfilled in Jesus. Read Isaiah 53 for a heavy prophecy about his death for us.

The New Testament begins with the four Gospels: Matthew, Mark, Luke and John. They are 'portraits' of Jesus rather than 'photographs'. Each writer selects his own special perspective on our Lord's birth, ministry, death and resurrection. They are either eyewitnesses to the events they record or immediate friends of eyewitnesses, who do their homework before writing (see Luke 1:1–4). The Gospels are particularly amazing because they capture the words and actions of Jesus as he actually lived, and climax with his death on the cross and his resurrection from the dead. In each Gospel he is shown to be the eternal Son of God who became fully human like us, going through all we go through yet never blowing it ('sinning'). 'For we do not have a high priest who is unable to sympathise with our weaknesses, but we have one who has been tempted in every way, just as we are – yet was without sin' (Hebrews 4:15).

The book of Acts shows us how Jesus' mission was passed on to his disciples, how the church grew, and how what the Holy Spirit did through Jesus he continued to do through these men and women. This builds us up to believe that he can do the same things through us today.

Most of the rest of the New Testament contains letters. Paul, who gave up persecuting Christians and spent the rest of his life winning people to Jesus, experiencing God's power and starting churches, wrote 13 of them. Other apostles, like James, Peter and John, added theirs. These are windows into the early church. They are sharpening and vibrant encouragements which are relevant and radical today.

Here we see that these new Christians struggle with the same problems we have and find that Jesus is the answer to every question (read Paul's letter to the Philippians to see this). For deep teaching on the gospel read Romans and Galatians (salvation isn't what we do, it is what Jesus has done – made real by his Spirit and our family life together). For a simple study of the Christian life, read 1 John (about holy love). For practical wisdom on how to live, read James. To learn how Jesus fulfils the Old Testament priesthood and sacrificial system, read Hebrews. To be ready for Jesus' return, read 1 and 2 Thessalonians.

The last book of the Bible (Revelation) contains

heavy visions of the conflict between God and the devil. While the battle rages on earth, the saints sing in heaven. The outcome is sure: Jesus reigns and will bring in a whole new order – the final judgement and restoration of the whole universe to God's great plan and purpose.

Throughout the Bible the themes are the same, yet we're carried through a rollercoaster of experiences and images of God the Creator, Redeemer, Father and Friend.

But where should we start? You could read a psalm and pray it in your own words. Or you could read a chapter in the Gospels and ask Jesus to help you to know him better. Think over what he says and does, thank him for what you see and learn. Ask him to make you more like himself.

You can also read passages and books for help with your own problems. James and Proverbs have good stuff on gossiping. Romans 8 tells us how to live a new life in the Spirit. You can look up a single word in a Bible concordance and find all the places where it is used. 'Hope', for example, will give you a lot to look forward to. 'Faith' will build you up for the present. 'Love' will put you in the centre of God's heart. The *Life Application Study Bible* is a big help in understanding what the message of the Bible is all about in everyday language. Get a modern translation like the NIV (New International Version) or NLT (New Living Translation).

Finding time!

Obviously we all live busy lives, but it really is possible for quiet times to become a simple and natural part of your everyday routine – it may just take a bit of discipline! The first thing is to be realistic about how much time you can set aside each day; this will determine whether you read a verse, a paragraph, a chapter or an entire book. If you can set aside time each day, it can make a real difference to your growth and also to the way you react in the situations you face daily.

I know that when I regularly spend time with God and the Bible it totally transforms my reactions to things. Take today, for example. We have just moved house and decided to employ a tree surgeon to cut down some trees in order to get a bit more sunshine in our garden. Right in the middle of the tree-cutting, my new next door neighbour came round. She was not very happy and started to give specific instructions as to what we could and couldn't do with our trees. This was slightly annoying as we had gone through all the proper channels and were cutting them in compliance with council rules. I couldn't believe someone could get that upset about some greenery, but she really was devastated that her view of our house had been affected!

Unfortunately, Matt (the diplomat in the Redman family) is away, so I had to deal with Mrs Moaner alone! To my surprise I initially managed to stay calm and be polite while ushering her off the premises. But once I got indoors I became more and more enraged! In fact by the time I spoke to Matt I was furious. I decided that the next time I saw her I would say something really rude and horrible, and tell her just what I thought of her. I looked out of the window at her house and hoped for a rematch soon! Then I picked up my Bible and decided to have a quiet time before work. I turned to the book of Proverbs and my mouth dropped open!

With his mouth the godless destroys his neighbour, but through knowledge the righteous escape. (Proverbs 11:9)

'Love your neighbour . . .'

A man who lacks judgment derides his neighbour, but a man of understanding holds his tongue. (Proverbs 11:12)

In some people's eyes I had every right to tear her to shreds for her rudeness, but not in God's. Wisdom and godliness say hold your tongue. Imagine if I had retaliated! To fall into a dispute with our neighbours in the first few months of living here would not be wise or appropriate – first, because we are Christians and second because we hope to live here for some time! I sighed and thanked God for his wonderful wisdom and his gentle rebuke. I love the way God speaks to me so directly through the Bible in my everyday, ordinary life.

When and where

There is no such thing as the perfect time or place for a quiet time, but God can speak to us powerfully and specifically anywhere and anytime. Only you will know what suits you best. I am a bit of a morning person, so it works best for me to grab some time before breakfast while everyone else is sleeping. When I lived in a house with four other girls there was never a quiet moment, so we used to put up a 'Do not disturb' sign on the door or nip into the bathroom if we were having a quiet time and did not want to be interrupted. (By the way, God is not legalistic and will not love you any less if things are crazy and you don't manage to get a quiet time. Please don't forget grace!)

Quiet times don't have to start at 4 am or last for an hour – they are much simpler than that. Just like eating breakfast or applying make-up, they can become a quick and easy but essential part of our day!

To finish this chapter I've put together three different types of quiet time. The best one for you will depend on how much time you have. Each section includes a simple framework that is easy to follow and that includes study notes and books should you want to go a bit deeper. I hope it helps.

Small (5 minutes)

Start: Read a verse such as Proverbs 16:28: 'A gossip separates close friends', or Psalm 139:23: 'Search me, O God, and know my heart; test me and know my anxious thoughts. See if there is any offensive way in me, and lead me in the way everlasting.'

Stop: Now pray through the verse. What does it mean to you? Have you gossiped or been gossiped about? What do you want to say to God about it? Is there anything on your heart that you are worried about, or is there something bugging you that you need to say sorry for or tell God about? Talk to him now.

Wait: Just because you only have time for a small quiet time today doesn't mean it has to be a one-way conversation. You still have time to listen, so spend a few minutes just waiting to hear God. It is often handy to keep a pen and paper handy so you can write down any thoughts or verses that come to mind. Even if you've waited and not heard anything specific, ask him to give you peace and strength for today.

Other good bits to read during a small quiet time are verses from Ephesians, Philippians, Matthew, Mark, Luke, John, 1 John or Jude.

Helpful resources

Book: *Piercing Proverbs* by Melody Carson.
Study guide: *Fresh* featuring The Tribe.

Medium (10–15 minutes)

Start: Because you've got a bit more time, why not try reading a couple of paragraphs from somewhere like Titus 2? Here is a little section from *The Message*:

> We're being shown how to turn our backs on a godless, indulgent life, and how to take on a God-filled, God-honoring life. This new life is starting right now, and is whetting our appetites for the glorious day when our great God and Savior, Jesus Christ, appears. He offered himself as a sacrifice to free us from a dark, rebellious life into this good, pure life, making us a people he can be proud of, energetic in goodness.

Stop: This passage shows us that God is changing us from being people who are consumed with sin and ourselves to people who are full of him. Stop and read these verses through again. What areas in your life has God changed for the good? Now what areas do you think still need to be addressed in order for you to honour God? Write a list of anything that comes to mind.

Wait: Now look over your list. Thank God for the things he has done in your life already – it is always good to stop and recognise the hand of God on your life. Next spend some time praying and commit to him the things that you still struggle with, then ask him to help you.

Other good bits to read during a medium quiet time are chunks from Colossians, Hebrews, Genesis 1–11, Daniel, Ruth, Esther or 1 and 2 Timothy.

Helpful resources

Book: *The Site: Daily Hits on God's Word* compiled by Craig Borlase (Hodder, 2000).
Study guide: 1Timothy and Titus: *Fighting the Good Fight* by John Stott (IVP, 1998).

Large (15–30 minutes)

Start: You have heaps of time, so why not try reading a chapter from Romans? Here's an extract from Romans 2:12:

> If you sin without knowing what you're doing, God takes that into account. But if you sin knowing full well what you're doing, that's a different story entirely. Merely hearing God's law is a waste of time if you don't do what he commands. Doing, not hearing, is what makes the difference with God. (*The Message*)

Stop: Why not find a study guide for the book of Romans and see if you can get a better insight into what Paul is writing? Through learning, we can reach a deeper level of understanding God's laws and God's character.

Wait: Have you been hearing but not doing? Spend some time being quiet and see if you hear an answer.

Now finish by praying through the things this passage has shown you about God and about your own life, and then just worship him for a while. Stick on a CD that will help you to concentrate and meet with God.

Other good bits to read during a large quiet time are chapters from Acts, Galatians, Isaiah, 1 and 2 Corinthians, 1 and 2 Samuel and Revelation.

Helpful resources

Book: *You've Got Mail* by Stephen Travis.
Study guide: *Cover to Cover* by Selwyn Hughes and Trevor Partridge.

Where I found Help When . . .

This section is a selection of inspiring and wise words from big sistas around the globe. I pray it will spur you on to pick up the big book and find God's wisdom for yourself.

Annie Flack

Don't let anyone look down on you because you are

young, but set an example for the believers in speech, in life, in love, in faith and in purity. (1 Timothy 4:12)

When I became a Christian at the age of 14, this was one of the first Bible verses I read. I loved the idea of not letting anyone look down on me because of my age. It was quite a while later before I paid much attention to the second half of the verse, and realised I actually had a responsibility. Instead of just walking around knowing I was just as good as any of the Christian oldies, I was actually called to live as an example to them. I was humbled and encouraged that God might even want my life to be an example for others: 'Set an example for the believers in speech, in life, in love, in faith and in purity.' I love the fact that God doesn't wait for us to grow old before he asks anything of us. He wants to use us in all of our lives, no matter how old, or young, we are.

Lou Fellingham

Therefore, since we have a great high priest who has gone through the heavens, Jesus the Son of God, let us hold firmly to the faith we profess. For we do not have a high priest who is unable to sympathise with our weaknesses, but we have one who has been tempted in every way, just as we are – yet was without sin. Let us then approach the throne of grace with confidence, so that we may receive mercy and find grace to help us in our time of need. (Hebrews 4:14–16)

This scripture has so helped me because it has made me realise that I don't have to have everything sorted before I come to God. Sometimes I've felt that I can't speak to God, or he won't understand, or that I have to spend a certain number of hours reading my Bible before I can come to him. But that's not what it says! It doesn't say that once I've got everything sorted then I can come to him. It says that as I come to him I receive the mercy and grace to help me in my time of need.

Shelley Giglio

So do not fear, for I am with you; do not be dismayed, for I am your God. I will strengthen you and help you; I will uphold you with my righteous right hand. (Isaiah 41:10)

One of the verses that has meant the most to me was

learned back when I was quite young. I was 13 years old and attended a school that had great diversity in the background of the students. I was quite intimidated by the school's size and the confronting nature of most of the students. One time, several of the students were bullying me because they believed I had been involved in something that I had not. I was terrified. At the age of 13, I learned a priceless lesson about the faithfulness of God. I memorised the verse above and quoted it to myself for days as the taunting continued. I was not harmed, I overcame, and I learned that day to lean on the word of God for encouragement, comfort and support in times of great need. The truth truly set me free. I still need it as desperately today as I did then!

Darlene Zschech

> You shaped me first inside, then out;
> You formed me in my mother's womb.
> I thank You, High God – You're breathtaking!
> Body and soul I am marvellously made!
> I worship in adoration – what a creation! (Psalm 139)

I became a Christian when I was 15 years old. My

family had split and somehow I found myself taking on a lot of the blame and a tremendous amount of guilt. My formative years had become my worst nightmare – not the perfect picture of home and family I'd always dreamed of. Then I met Jesus.

His word, his promise, his overwhelming love started to redefine in my heart who I was, and most importantly *whose I was*, and through spending time reading the Bible God started healing my heart and making me new. My life is truly miraculous and I can confidently say that he's turned my mourning into dancing.

The scripture that spoke so clearly into the core of me at that time was Psalm 139. It tells beautifully of God knowing me inside and out before I was born. That he made me wonderfully complex to bring him glory all the days of my life. It says that every single day of my life was recorded in his book. (I would *so* love to see that book!) And in verse 24 it says, 'Point out anything in me that offends you, and lead me along the path of everlasting life.'

So there you have it – my focus from those days to this is that I love my God with all I am, and he will always find me ready to worship and obey. May I be known as someone who loves her Lord and lifts the lives of people. I discovered that when you allow God to transform your heart and life as a young person, your life will flourish in ways that you never even dared to dream about.

Kara Townsend

> Love is patient, love is kind. It does not envy, it does not boast, it is not proud. It is not rude, it is not self-seeking, it is not easily angered, it keeps no record of wrongs. Love does not delight in evil, but rejoices with the truth. It always protects, always trusts, always hopes, always perseveres. (1 Corinthians 13:4–7)

When I was twelve years old, I sat on my bed and suddenly realised that I wanted to get to know God for myself. So I started reading my Bible in Genesis, but quickly lost interest. As I stumbled upon this well-known passage, I actually *felt*, for the first time in my life, that I wanted to be like Jesus. I decided to break down the qualities of love and try to follow them in my life. I made a chart with a different 'personality' of love to work on each day (e.g. patience, then kindness), and began to see God soften my heart towards my brothers, my parents and my annoying classmates as I tried to apply his word to my life. I didn't have a clue what I was doing, but I had to start somewhere. Somehow, though, God used it to bring to mind the qualities he is still growing in me today.

Christy Wimber

I came to you in weakness and fear, and with much trembling. My message and my preaching were not with wise and persuasive words, but with a demonstration of the Spirit's power, so that your faith might not rest on men's wisdom, but on God's power. (1 Corinthians 2:3–5)

A few years ago I started putting together worship events around the world. I always used to make other people get on the stage and do the 'up front' stuff. I preferred to lead 'behind the scenes', where it felt safer. So when my father-in-law started telling me I needed to get out there and speak to the people, my first response was, 'No way!' I had always been around so many gifted people that I really thought that what I had to offer could never be as good, or as neatly polished. However, I did start speaking and ministering, and slowly over the years it's become easier.

I remember one occasion when I had to go out and lead a ministry time in front of a few thousand people and I was literally shaking. But the Lord showed me the above verse and reassured me that all I needed to do was show up and look for what he was doing. It doesn't matter how stupid or weak I feel. What matters is that I do what God asks of me, and keep looking to him. So often we put too much pressure on ourselves and what we have to offer. I believe that the weaker I feel, the better it can be – less of me and more of Jesus.

Andy Arganda

> Come to me, all you who are weary and burdened, and I will give you rest. Take my yoke upon you and learn from me, for I am gentle and humble in heart, and you will find rest for your souls. For my yoke is easy and my burden is light. (Matthew 11:28)

This scripture has always been a great source of hope, and brought comfort to me. There have been a number of times in my life where loved ones around me have suffered terrible illnesses. My youngest sister was diagnosed with leukaemia when she was two-and-a-half years old (she is now 19 and completely healthy). My brother died of a chromosome disease. A very dear friend of mine died of cancer a couple of years ago, and most recently my other sister was diagnosed with multiple sclerosis.

During each of these scary times of wondering what the diagnosis and outcome were going to be, I was reminded of this great scripture. As I poured my heart out to Jesus, he was faithful in carrying my burden and I managed to find peace of mind and rest in him. The Bible never ceases to amaze me. Daily I come across new truths and promises written years and years ago, but still so valid and true for what is happening in my life today.

Ali MacInnes

My grace is sufficient for you, for my power is made perfect in weakness. (2 Corinthians 12:9)

For it is by grace you have been saved, through faith – and this not from yourselves, it is the gift of God – not by works, so that no-one can boast. (Ephesians 2:8–9)

A few years ago I went through a time of depression.

Not 'having-a-bad-day' depressed but months of pain leading up to medication and counselling, and a few suicidal thoughts along the way. I had nothing to look forward to. Over a period of time I lost all confidence, couldn't cope with normal life, felt frightened in crowds and lost all sense of a hope and a future. It was a really horrible period of tears and emptiness, and at the time I couldn't imagine things would ever be any different.

During this time I found it really hard to read my Bible and pray. I chatted with a couple of wise friends who'd had experience with the whole depression thing. They told me that this is common and that I needed to remember there are times in life when it's OK simply to rest in God's presence. It was a hard lesson to learn. On the one hand I felt guilty for not reading my Bible, and on the other I just knew I couldn't. I was so lethargic and couldn't really concentrate on anything, so I had to give in. In the end the lesson I learned was this: the Father's love for me is not, and will never be, based on what I have or haven't done – past, present or future. God wasn't yelling at me in my depressed state, 'Why aren't you reading your Bible? How dare you? Get on with life and stop moping about!' Instead he quietened me with his love, speaking to me gently and tenderly.

And Jesus did heal me – he began a process that to be honest is still going on today. As I look back on that time of depression I can't pretend that it wasn't horrible, but neither can I bring myself to regret it. It was a refining time; a time to clear out some of the mess that had been building up over the years. God used that painful season to show me who I am in him, what I'm called to, and that my life and security can only come from being firmly rooted in him.

Diane Louise Jordan

> And a voice from heaven said, 'This is my Son, whom I love; with him I am well pleased.' (Matthew 3:17)

I love this scripture because it really helped me to understand how much God loves me. Jesus has just been baptised and up until this point all we know is that he was a carpenter. His ministry hasn't even begun, and yet God says that he *loves* Jesus and he is well pleased with his Son. This is exactly how God loves us! He loves us and is well pleased with us simply because we're his sons and daughters – and not because of our efforts. Over the years this scripture has encouraged me to realise that our perfect Father (who doesn't make mistakes) designed each of us to be uniquely as we are. And if we're good enough for God, we must be good enough for the world.

Carrie Grant

> She gets up while it is still dark; she provides food for her family and portions for her servant girls. She considers a field and buys it; out of her earnings she plants a vineyard. (Proverbs 31:15–16)

I love these verses because they are so empowering for women today. Sometimes people think that to be a Christian woman all you have to do is sit at home all day in dodgy sandals, praying for a husband and then bearing him some children, and then you'll be totally satisfied. There's nothing wrong with this. But the woman in Proverbs is a woman who provides for and takes care of her family and staff – and is a property developer too! Now for me that's inspiring and totally cool!

Debby Wright

> Love the Lord your God with all your heart . . . and
> your neighbour as yourself. (Luke 10:27)

I have a tendency to become overly introspective and
self-absorbed, and the best antidote to all that stuff in
my life is to start living by these two commandments.
There is simply nothing more fun and wonderful than
being free to worship God – it completely lifts me out
of my introspection and places me firmly before the
throne of God. When I think of others and try to
serve them, I begin to feel relationally healthy and full
of purpose. Putting these two commandments into
practice practically settles who I am and what I am
for. It's no wonder Jesus said that all the Law and the
Prophets hang on these two commandments.

Cindy Reithmeir

> In all their distress he too was distressed, and the angel
> of his presence saved them. In his love and mercy he
> redeemed them; he lifted them up and carried them all
> the days of old. (Isaiah 63:9)

I came across this scripture in the middle of a family crisis. I could not see any way around or past the situation. I was in constant turmoil over the thought of my family being torn apart, and our relationships being damaged beyond repair. I was beginning to understand that I was not in control and the only way we could survive was if God rescued us.

I was grateful when I read this verse because it reminded me that God felt my fear and anguish as deeply as I was feeling them. He was ready to come to me in love, mercy and redemption, and he was willing and able to lift me up and carry me through each day. My one and only assurance in life is Jesus, and this was one of the times when I was reminded of what a great gift the promise of his presence is in times of difficulty.

Rachel Fellingham

> Don't let anyone look down on you because you are young, but set an example for the believers in speech, in life, in love, in faith and in purity. (1 Timothy 4:12)

When I was 15, this verse in 1 Timothy really encouraged me. Quite often people think you have to be experienced or ancient for God to be able to use you. I wanted to be able to do things for God, but people don't always take you seriously when you are young. This verse says that God can use you as a young person to be an example, even to older people. It really helped me to go for it and not worry about what others thought of me.

Sarah

Now faith is being sure of what we hope for and certain of what we do not see. (Hebrews 11:1)

Faith in God doesn't change when things get difficult. As this verse tells us, faith is the conviction of things not seen. I have faith in who God is. I have faith in his goodness and kindness, his justice and his love. I have faith that though things may get worse, he will never change.

I grew up in a Christian family, but from the age of two until I was 13, I was abused at home by my step-dad. I never told anyone about the abuse, but eventually found a way to move in with my father and his wife. At first things went pretty well, but my dad became addicted to alcohol and prescription drugs.

When I was 18, two days before Christmas, I received a phone call telling me he had choked and slipped into a coma. Two days later, on Christmas day, he died.

Where is God when we suffer? The answer is that he is as close as he is when we're on top of the world. Suffering isn't what draws us away from God. In many ways, it can be what draws us the closest. When we suffer, we're forced to remove all of our faith in the 'good life' we can see around us, and instead place our faith and hope in God alone.

Kate Virgo

> Delight yourself in the Lord and he will give you the desires of your heart. (Psalm 37:4)

I grew up in a Christian family, which I appreciated and enjoyed until I was about 17. I then felt as though a lot of decisions had been made for me, and wondered if I was only a Christian because of my upbringing. I became convinced Christianity was a bunch of rules that you had to follow which were meant to stop you having fun. I panicked and began to rebel against my parents and the church in order to search for what I thought was the real meaning of life.

I ended up travelling around Australia – which I loved – but all I was really doing was putting off decisions about my future.

Once back in England I was restless, unhappy and felt very unclear about the future. Then at Christmas my parents asked me to go to church with them. I went feeling very cynical, but it actually wasn't too bad. A lady there spoke about God's love, and how it was unconditional. Over the next few months I was on a journey of actually getting to know God and realising the truth that we are happiest when we are in God's will. He knows what is best for us and knows that we are truly fulfilled when we are walking close to him. God doesn't watch over us, waiting for us to make our next mistake, but lovingly guides us and offers forgiveness when we blow it.

Annie Flack

Let us then approach the throne of grace with confidence, so that we may receive mercy and find grace to help us in our time of need. (Hebrews 4:16)

So often in life I find myself shying away from God's presence. When I know I've not been living the way he asks me to, or when I haven't spent time with him for a while, instead of running to him I try and hide away. This verse has reminded me many times that drawing close to God isn't about coming to get a well-deserved smack! When we come towards his throne, we find grace, love and mercy. When I remember this, I'm much quicker to turn myself around and draw near to him. When I was 15, some friends and I turned this verse into a little song so we could remember it. It was a bit sad, but it's been amazing how many times the song has come into my mind just at the right times, reminding me to come confidently into his presence, knowing that I'll always be met with grace and mercy.

Renske Aerts

> For as the heavens are high above the earth, so great is His mercy toward those who fear Him; as far as the east is from the west, so far has He removed our transgressions from us. (Psalm 103:11–12, NKJV)

As a young teenager I struggled with feelings of guilt. I guess I was a bit of a rebel. I just didn't want to conform to the 'rules' of Christianity, and I lived on the edge, sometimes falling off the wrong side. I'd experienced from some people a type of faith that was cold and without mercy. But there was a radical turn in my spiritual life when God revealed to me through the Bible that his mercy is without end. As far as the east is from the west . . . that's even far enough for me!

Ali MacInnes

> Being confident of this, that he who began a good work in you will carry it on to completion until the day of Christ Jesus. (Philippians 1:6)

This is a verse that I love to come back to time and time again – particularly when I'm struggling with the same old sin in my life, or when I feel weighed down by hurts that I so desperately long to be free from. This verse is God's promise to me that he will not give up on me. He won't abandon me, get tired of me or stop forgiving me, but he *will* carry on the good work he started. It is God, not me, who changes me to make me more like his Son.

The Unquenchable Worshipper

by Matt Redman

This book is about a kind of worshipper:

Unquenchable. Undivided. Unpredictable.

On a quest to bring glory and pleasure to God, these worshippers will not allow themselves to be distracted or defeated:

Unstoppable. Undignified. Undone.

Worshippers who long for their hearts, lives and songs to be the kind of offerings God is looking for.

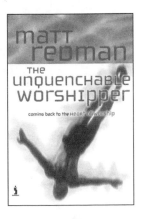

'This is unashamedly a book about God and living a devoted life in His presence. Worship is *about* God, *to* God and *for* God. *The Unquenchable Worshipper* shouts this truth out loud.'

Mike Pilavachi, Soul Survivor

survivor